THE GOLDEN RULE

THE GOLDEN RULE

A Universal Ethic

by

H.T.D. Rost

GEORGE RONALD
OXFORD

George Ronald, Publisher
46 High Street, Kidlington, Oxford OX5 2DN

British Library Cataloguing in Publication Data

Rost, H.T.D
    The golden rule : a universal ethic.
    1. Theology, Doctrinal—Comparative
    studies
    I. Title
    291.2   BL85

    ISBN 0-85398-226-0
    ISBN 0-85398-227-9 Pbk

Typeset by Sunrise Setting, Torquay, Devon
Printed and bound in Great Britain by Billing & Sons Limited, Worcester

Contents

Preface

'The teaching that we should treat others as we ourselves would wish to be treated, an ethic variously repeated in all the great religions . . . sums up the moral attitude, the peace-inducing aspect, extending through these religions irrespective of their place or time of origin; it also signifies an aspect of unity which is their essential virtue, a virtue mankind in its disjointed view of history has failed to appreciate.' These words, addressed to the peoples of the world in October 1985 by the Universal House of Justice of the Bahá'í Faith in its inspiring appeal *The Promise of World Peace*, could stand as the *leitmotif* of this book.

The Golden Rule has interested thinkers for centuries, but although it has been much discussed, it has seldom been treated extensively or in depth in the literature. This is quite surprising in view of the obvious importance of the Rule.

In attempting to study the Golden Rule the present writer was particularly encouraged by the following words of 'Abdu'l-Bahá, written to an individual:

Thou hast directed all thy thoughts toward acquiring light from the realms of mystery. So long as the thoughts of an individual are scattered he will achieve no results, but if his thinking be concentrated on a single point wonderful will be the fruits thereof.

One cannot obtain the full force of the sunlight when it is cast on a flat mirror, but once the sun shineth upon a concave mirror, or on a lens that is convex, all its heat will be concentrated on a single point, and that one point will burn the hottest. Thus is it necessary to focus one's thinking on a single point so that it will become an effective force.*

And

All blessings are divine in origin, but none can be compared with this power of intellectual investigation and research, which is an eternal gift producing fruits of unending delight.†

I have had no delusions about the subtleties, complexities and pitfalls to be faced while exploring this subject. In attempting to present an overview of the topic, I have had to blend materials from various sacred books as well as studies of comparative religion, history of religion, morality, ethics, philosophy, education, psychology and psychiatry while adding a pinch of personal experience. I do not pretend to be expert in these fields. For instance, I am not a trained philosopher and have no pretensions to be one; therefore, I did not go into many detailed philosophical discussions and controversies about the Rule. But I have clearly seen that much of the available literature demonstrates the links between the Rule and religion.

Each writer brings along his own personal baggage: his particular background and experience. Being a Bahá'í, the present writer is more familiar with the Bahá'í Faith than any other religion. But a Bahá'í who writes a book like this one is in no way committed to a one-sided position. I have made a conscious, concerted attempt to present all the religions treated in the book as openly and fairly as possible and even in a few instances have made reference to the views of humanist or existentialist thinkers. With this in mind, I have drawn upon the expertise of a wide variety of people to read and comment on the manuscript. These include

* 'Abdu'l-Bahá, *Selections from the Writings of 'Abdu'l-Bahá*, pp. 110–11.
† 'Abdu'l-Bahá, *The Promulgation of Universal Peace*, p. 50.

persons who are familiar in particular with traditional religions, Hinduism, Zoroastrianism, Judaism, Christianity, Islám, Sikhism and the Bahá'í Faith; persons who have a good knowledge of several faiths; and individuals knowledgeable in philosophy. Those who very kindly read and offered suggestions include Mr Habib Behi; Dr Kamuyu-wa-Kang'ethe; Mr Badru Kateregga; Mr Justus Mbae; Mrs Ridvan Mobedzadeh; my respected father-in-law, Dr H. M. Munje; Mrs Gursharan Surjit Narula; Professor Raphael Njoroge; Rev. Dr Zablon Nthamburi; Professor V. N. Verma; and Dr K. Wambari. Mrs Deborah Christensen and Mr Ted Groenewegen rendered a particularly valuable service by reading and evaluating the entire manuscript. Some of these persons were my colleagues on the academic staff in the Department of Philosophy and Religious Studies and the Department of Educational Foundations at Kenyatta University College. One of my postgraduate students, Mr Joseph Sukwianomb, and four other friends, Mr Ted Groenewegen, Dr Kamuyu-wa-Kang'ethe, Mr Barnabas Kipkorir and Mrs Donna Taylor provided valuable statements that are incorporated in the text. Mr Ralph Wagner also kindly provided a version of one 'Golden Rule' statement. Mrs Nancy Phillips gave helpful information. Special appreciation is due to the Continental Board of Counsellors for Central and Eastern Africa for kindly making available valuable source material and to Dr May Hofman Ballerio, who edited the book.

My wife, Radha, discussed aspects of the subject with me many times and gave a number of valuable suggestions. Her sincere interest and help contributed substantially to the completion of the book. Our three sons, John, Paul and Collis, were also actively involved in a family effort to understand the Rule more thoroughly and to attempt to see its application in everyday life.

The reader's attention is drawn to certain particular

problems that will be noticeable as he reads the book. Firstly, although I have attempted to take as universal an approach to the subject as possible, in certain chapters I have had to rely heavily on Western sources, as these were more readily available. Secondly, the reader will note different translations of a given Golden Rule statement here and there in the text. Thirdly, I have tried throughout to make a clear distinction between my own personal views and (1) the accepted tenets of particular faiths or (2) some authorities' understanding of aspects of particular faiths. If I have failed to do so clearly in certain cases, apologies are in order.

An attempt was made to overcome one apparent common shortcoming in the literature on the Golden Rule: the 'lifting' of statements of the Rule from context. Often, such practice is a barrier to fuller understanding of the meaning and significance of given statements. The reader will therefore find that, particularly where primary sources are quoted, statements of the Rule are given within their contexts. That I was limited to using citations of the Rule from secondary sources in some cases is regrettable but, in the circumstances, unavoidable.

One final note to the reader. *The Golden Rule* is intended not as a book to read quickly and skim through, but to be savoured and pondered over, in the hope that the ideas and ideals therein will lead to constructive action.

Panchgani, India
November 1985

Introduction

'Troops Killing Civilians.' 'Lawyers Fight With Police-men.' 'Accountant Steals Money.' 'Save Our Filthy Town.' Today's newspapers proclaim the severe moral problems rampant in the world. We also experience them in our everyday lives. Shoghi Effendi, Guardian of the Bahá'í Faith and an astute observer of world affairs, warned:

The signs of moral downfall . . . are too numerous and too patent for even a superficial observer of the state of present-day society to fail to notice. The spread of lawlessness, of drunkenness, of gambling, and of crime; the inordinate love of pleasure, of riches, and other earthly vanities; the laxity in morals, revealing itself in the irresponsible attitude towards marriage, in the weakening of parental control, in the rising tide of divorce, in the deterioration in the standard of literature and of the press, and in the advocacy of theories that are the very negation of purity, of morality and chastity – these evidences of moral decadence, invading both the East and the West, permeating every stratum of society, and instilling their poison in its members of both sexes, young and old alike, blacken still further the scroll upon which are inscribed the manifold transgressions of an unrepentant humanity.[1]

Effective character education is all too often non-existent. Moral decay's partners are a rampant materialism and a devastating decline in the influence of religion. One of the fundamental characteristics of virtually every religion is that it incorporates a code of ethics. Historically, the religions of the world have been a fertile source of moral and ethical principles and practices. But today we live in '. . . an age which has lost moral clarity and religious conviction'.[2]

The causes of the 'weakening of the pillars of religion' throughout the globe are too complex for us to review here. To many people the older religions seem outdated when faced by the manifold, complex moral problems plaguing the modern world. Equally, the modern secular approach to morality and moral education seems grossly inadequate and ineffective to many.

Despite a widespread rising tide of awareness of the need for religious unity and understanding, some followers of religions today persist with bloody persecutions of the adherents of other faiths, irrational contempt for other faiths, and devastating wars in which religious prejudices are conspicuous. Sects within religions are often at loggerheads with each other. All this contributes to the decline of religion and lack of a common front against the real enemy – moral degradation.

I

Religion, Morality and Ethics

Religion, morality and ethics cannot be entirely isolated from each other in neat compartments. The relationship between ethics and morality is generally recognised by philosophers. One scholar briefly outlined his view of this relationship:

In general, *ethics* refers to values in the context of human behavior or conduct. An ethical act is one which has reference to good or desirable behavior. The term *moral* is often used synonymously with *ethical*, but there are a number of distinctions between them. One difference, discussed by Aristotle, is that while *ethics* refers to the *theory* of behavior, *moral* refers to the *practice*. In another sense, the term *moral* refers to any judgment of good or bad arising from a social matrix.[1]

Therefore, on the surface at least, morality may be viewed simply in terms of practical activities in the daily lives of human beings everywhere. A normal person faces moral problems and makes moral judgements virtually every day of his life from childhood onwards. If he were to keep a record of the nature, importance and frequency of his judgements of good or bad, right or wrong, during a single day, even though the exercise might be far from easy, the results could be very enlightening and a spur towards improvement.

Religions have been powerful instruments moulding

moral values in the societies in which they have been found. Many thinkers today, even in this irreligious world, maintain that ethics, morality and religion are so closely intertwined that one cannot be studied or understood without the other.

Shoghi Effendi's secretary wrote on his behalf that

no sound ethic can exist and become effective unless based on revealed religion. To dissociate ethics from religion is to render the former not only void of any firm foundation but without the necessary driving power.[2]

Sadly, many older religions seem to have lost the vital spark that reflected so brightly in praiseworthy moral conduct among the faithful of the past. On the other hand, 'When a religion is vital and creative, the moral conduct of its followers provides evidences of its living power.'[3]

We usually think of morality in terms of our relationships with other human beings. I may feel that I can keep my own good or bad thoughts to myself, but when those thoughts are expressed in acts involving other people, moral issues are often involved. Moreover, I may consistently neglect the possibility that my thoughts have an effect on others, even if not overtly expressed, without my realising it. This, too, raises moral problems.

At any rate, some thinkers feel that relationships with others are at the basis of morality. For example:

Indeed, awareness of others, feeling for others, and therefore concern for others are the basic hall-marks of all morality. It is living in society that gives rise to morality and makes it necessary.[4]

They think that most of the moral decisions we face inevitably will involve other people. However, others have claimed that the directly social aspect of morality may be stressed too much and that the direct identification of the person with the social world is not the sole root of morality.[5]

But social institutions and organisations are very much involved in moral relationships, one example being relations between modern nations – often in a pitifully sad state of affairs at present. National morality is, obviously, a much more complex matter than moral relationships between two individuals, yet at least some principles of ethics and morals expounded by the great religions and philosophies apply to both. In future, with the likely development of a world state, moral relationships between nations may change considerably. Global morality could take on a whole new dimension, and ethical and moral principles would then have to fit the needs of a new age. Further, in the words of the Christian religious philosopher Pierre Teilhard de Chardin,

In *morals*, I take it that the time has come when (without even in the least degree rationalising the Christian virtues) we must nevertheless examine in what ways they harmonise with the experiential orientation of human progress . . .

From another angle, the ever vaster organisations that are being formed (or disclosed) in the World are tending to produce a new category of duties; and room must be made for these alongside the old commandments. Morality has hitherto been individualistic (the relations of individuals to individuals). In future more explicit emphasis will have to be laid on Man's obligations to collective bodies and even to the Universe: on political duties, social duties, international duties – on (if I may be allowed the expression) cosmic duties . . .[6]

We cannot, like ostriches, stick our heads into the sand and refuse to recognise that the world is changing rapidly. In the past, moral relationships existed between the members of relatively small, often isolated social groups, often with one set of moral obligations for relationships with one's own limited group and another set for 'outsiders'. There may even have been little or no moral obligation felt towards 'outsiders' at all. In the one case, the stage was set for rewards, brotherhood and mutuality, while in the other, revenge, retribution and feuds were the order of the day.[7] But in the modern world a radical change is taking place as *to whom* we are to behave morally. Man is emerging from 'tribal brotherhood' through 'brotherhood within the nation' towards 'universal brotherhood'. Older, limited ties of clan, tribe, caste, class, etc. are disintegrating. The number and variety of persons and groups with whom individuals have moral relationships is proliferating every day as the world moves towards a greater degree of unity. The old set of moral obligations suited for relationships between 'us' as against those felt towards 'them' is badly in need of an overhaul.

Moral relationships can involve much more than just human beings: they can embrace the whole of creation – mineral, vegetable, animal, man, although the moral relationship between a man and a man is somewhat different from that between, for example, a man and a plant (see pp. 34–5 below). For instance, at present, environmentalists are attempting to formulate a global environmental ethic. In fact, moral relationships, as we shall see later, can very well involve both the natural and supernatural, divine revelators and God Himself. Such relationships are clearly set forth in such faiths as Hinduism, Zoroastrianism, Judaism, Christianity, Islám, Sikhism and the Bahá'í Faith.

The Golden Rule, being an ethical or moral principle or rule, must be understood within the totality of a given ethical system or a comparison of two or more ethical systems as well as in relationship to the development of good character, virtues and perfections such as love and truthfulness.

2

What is the Golden Rule?

If you were to ask your friend, 'What is the Golden Rule?' he might, if of Christian background, quote from the words of Jesus Christ recorded in Matthew, chapter 7, verse 12, in the Bible: 'All things whatsoever ye would that men should do to you, do ye even so to them.' But he is more likely to give you the popular version of the Rule: 'Do unto others as you would have them do unto you', or 'Do as you would be done by.' And your friend probably does not know that a very important teaching similar to Jesus' Golden Rule is attributed to Confucius: 'What you do not want done to yourself, do not do to others.'[1] In fact, it is likely that the term 'Golden Rule' is less familiar to people of non-Jewish and non-Christian backgrounds, as the term is usually associated with several statements in the Bible. Jews can refer to Leviticus 19:18: 'Thou shalt love thy neighbour as thyself' as an example of the principle. Many others do not have the slightest notion what the Golden Rule is.

As we shall see in detail later, the Golden Rule existed in the form of approximations to the saying of Jesus Christ long before his time. The term itself has been in use since about the seventeenth century, when the statements found in Matthew 7:12 and Luke 6:31 were designated as 'the Golden Rule' or 'the Golden Law',[2] but the origin of the term is obscure. It is a most flexible term, meaning a variety of things to different people – and its meaning continues to change with the passage of time. The reader will find that the various writers referred to in this book are not consistent with each other in applying the term; this is a very complex problem that is difficult to resolve. To some, it applies only to the statements in Matthew 7:12 and Luke 6:31 or, in addition, a few other places in the Bible, while to others (including the present writer) the term has a much wider application.

Golden Rule statements are found in virtually every major religion existing in the world today. Yet few writers have attempted to explain what these statements in the world's religions actually have in common. Robert Ernest Hume stated that eight systems of religion and philosophy from which he quoted Golden Rule statements in *The World's Living Religions* 'bid a person apply to his conduct [towards] other people the simple test whether he would like such treatment accorded to him'.[3]

(The present writer maintains that the 'test' is often not so 'simple'! Also, the Golden Rule, if understood in a broad sense, can be applied to more than 'people'.) This basic reciprocity, which is central in Matthew 7:12 above, is, however, very often linked with other injunctions such as this from the Zoroastrian *Dīnkard*:

This, too, that when affliction has come upon a good *man*, the effort of every one, for removing that affliction, should continue just as though it happened to himself.

And when a good *man* is beaten through malice, the effort of every one, in demanding compensation for him from the smiter, should continue just as though it happened to himself.[4]

Golden Rule statements may be addressed on a relatively narrow level to a particular individual (such as a king), on a wider level to a particular class of individuals (such as a group of disciples or the followers of a particular persuasion), or even to the whole of mankind. This issue may be complicated by the fact that particular statements that, on the surface, are addressed to individuals or groups may be interpreted to have a wider applicability. The Golden Rule may thus be applied on various levels – between individual and individual, between individual and group, between group and group, etc., up to the point where, as we shall see later, the context for the process may be the whole of reality.

The Golden Rule has both negative and positive forms. For example, Jesus Christ's injunction, 'Whatsoever ye would that men should do to you, do ye even so to them', is regarded as positive, while the Confucian precept, 'What you do not want done to yourself, do not do to others', is considered negative. Later we shall consider this whole issue in more detail. The negative formulation is to be distinguished from its denial: 'Do *not* do unto others as you would have them do unto you.' The Golden Rule of Jesus Christ also has particular and general interpretations or forms.[5] It may also be distinguished from what is termed its 'inversion': 'Do unto others as *they* would have you do unto them.'[6]

The precept 'Do as you are done by' is a form of the *lex talionis* (law of retaliation) and may be distinguished from the Golden Rule. We shall discuss this first in Chapter 4 on traditional religions and then in Chapter 11 on Judaism in which 'eye for eye, tooth for tooth' morality is considered. Also, we shall study in some detail the traditional formulation of different levels of reciprocity beginning on the 'lowest' level of the 'Iron Rule' of 'eye for eye, tooth for tooth' and continuing through the 'Tinsel Rule', the 'Silver Rule', the 'Golden Rule', and, at the highest level, either at the ultimate level of reciprocity or above it, the 'Rule of Love'.

The Golden Rule as it is broadly interpreted is said to

have various corollaries. These are not to be regarded as
Golden Rule statements as such but may follow or be
inferred from them. Such corollaries include, among other
things, exhortations to refrain from backbiting, to avoid ill-
natured criticism, to shun slander, etc. An example is found
in the following words contained in the Hindu holy book,
the *Mahābhārata*:

> Faults, mustard-small, of others, ye see well;
> Your own, as large as bél-fruit, ye see not.[7]

Occasionally the Golden Rule is confused with the
'Golden Mean'. Aristotle is said to be the author of the
Golden Mean. 'Everything in its place, and everything in
moderation; nothing too much . . . For example, *courage* is
the mean between *cowardice* and *rashness*.'[8]

The word 'Golden' in 'Golden Rule' expresses the high
status the 'Rule' deserves. But surprisingly, to many
scholars, the Golden Rule is not a rule at all. Some of them
refer to it as 'the so-called "Golden Rule"'. It has been
termed a principle, a principle of conduct, a good working
principle for moral conduct, a moral principle, an ethical
principle, a general principle, a universal principle for
human relationship, the supreme law of rational ethics, a
fundamental ethical truth, a moral precept, an epigram, a
maxim, an axiom, and so forth – as well as a rule, a general
rule, a rule of conduct, etc. No doubt these differences are
related to such factors as the scope of application of the term
in the mind of each individual writer. We shall see later how
the Golden Rule has close links with the development of
law in religion.

Many scholars refer to the Golden Rule as a principle.
One of the few to have written an article entirely devoted to
the subject, Marcus G. Singer, gave a rationale for
regarding it as a moral principle rather than a moral rule.

But what he probably had basically in mind was the biblical injunction in Matthew 7:12 and Luke 6:31.

Despite its name, the Golden Rule has to be understood as a moral principle, and not as a moral rule. That is to say, it does not, as does a moral rule, state of some specifically determined kind of action that it is right or wrong, or that it ought or ought not to be done. It rather sets forth, or has to be understood as setting forth, in abstract fashion, a method or procedure for determining the morality of a line of action, and thus is intended to provide a principle from which, or in accordance with which, if it is valid, more specific or concrete moral rules can be derived.[9]

But as we have already seen in the example from the *Dīnkard*, many authorities have interpreted the term in such a way that it not only 'sets forth, or has to be understood as setting forth, in abstract fashion, a method or procedure for determining the morality of a line of action', but also relates to 'some specifically determined kind of action that it is right or wrong, or that it ought or ought not to be done'. Thus, statements of the Golden Rule as broadly understood can combine the characteristics of a moral principle as viewed by Singer with those of a moral rule.

The student of religion (or of philosophy or education or psychiatry, for that matter) plumbs enormous depths when investigating and meditating about the Golden Rule. Singer remarked, 'There are problems connected with it of the utmost subtlety, worthy of the attention of even the most minute philosophers.'[10]

3

Comparative Religion and the Golden Rule

The student of comparative religion has the fortunate and, at present, uncommon opportunity of seeking out and savouring some of the world's most delicious fruits – humanity's common store of religious wisdom and guidance. His enjoyment of some of these fruits will be spoiled if, through prejudice and intolerance, through bigoted adherence to his own particular religion or sect, he decides before close investigation that some of those fruits will be far less delicious than others. The present writer, being a Bahá'í, has found the study of comparative religion to be a delight, an experience that has profoundly enriched his understanding and appreciation of some of the endless depths of his own faith as well as of the beauties of others. One can definitely gain insights into any one faith through some knowledge of others. For example, one's understanding of a Golden Rule statement from a particular religion is often much enriched through contemplation of and comparison with similar statements from other faiths, or by relating it to examples of the Golden Rule in practice from the literature of other faiths. An attempt to follow this practice has been made in this book, the results being left to the reader to judge.

The fact that the Bahá'í Faith upholds the principles of the oneness of religion and the elimination of all forms of prejudice (including religious prejudice) has also influenced the writer's point of view. He feels that loving understanding of others' beliefs promotes better relations with the followers of the world's creeds – as well as with those who profess no religion. To him, the student of comparative religion would do well to take to heart the words of Bahá'u'lláh, the founder of the Bahá'í Faith, when He enjoined His followers to

> consort with the followers of all religions in a spirit of friendliness and fellowship, to proclaim that which the Speaker on Sinai hath set forth and to observe fairness in all matters.
>
> They that are endued with sincerity and faithfulness should associate with all the peoples and kindreds of the earth with joy and radiance, inasmuch as consorting with people hath promoted and will continue to promote unity and concord, which in turn are conducive to the maintenance of order in the world and to the regeneration of nations. Blessed are such as hold fast to the cord of kindliness and tender mercy and are free from animosity and hatred.[1]

The principle of the oneness of religion is upheld by certain scholars, some of whom know little or nothing about the Bahá'í Faith. Works on comparative religion were produced by Muslim scholars hundreds of years ago. In the West, serious attention to the question of the oneness of religion in recent history goes back at least to the early nineteenth century, when intense study began of the religious depth and pluriformity of the non-Christian religions. Before that time, followers of a particular faith typically branded other religions as 'false'. But the science of comparative religion was searching for the 'essence of religion', an essence that was common to all religions and which was the connecting link between all of them.[2] Despite continued controversies up to the present, the search has yielded some significant results.

It is now a common conviction that the religions of the world do not present a disconnected and chaotic variety in which there is no perceivable unity . . . There is a general conviction of a certain regularity, but it has proven exceedingly difficult to arrive at a further pin-pointing of that regularity. Parallels are discovered in the forms of expression that different religions use. Similar problems come to the attention of students of different religions. Scholars have sought the 'common elements which come through various religions'.[3]

Of the greatest significance for our purposes, citations of the Golden Rule from various faiths have been used over and over again by writers when attempting to demonstrate those common features of the world's religions. For example, R. E. Hume, a scholar evidently of Christian background, presented what he felt were such common features:[4]

1. The belief in one supreme Being.
2. The claim of divine incarnation.
3. The claim of a supernatural origin of the founder.
4. The claim of divine revelation.
5. The claim of an inspired scripture.
6. The report of miracles wrought.
7. The principle of 'the Golden Rule'.
8. The recognition of an especially sacred community.
9. The hope of a universal religion.
10. The hopes and fears of a future life.
    (Each item was discussed in some detail.)

Some authorities would not agree completely with Hume's list.[5] The subtleties of this whole issue are outside the scope of our subject, but it must be obvious to the reader that one fundamental problem that must be tackled in this book is whether this broad, global study of the Golden Rule does, indeed, demonstrate that it *is* a common feature of religion – in fact, whether it is a universal feature of religion or not.

Some scholars have made the sweeping assertion that this noble teaching is to be found in *all* religions – in fact, in some instances, in *all* creeds *and* philosophies. In an 1894 publication, Thomas Henry Huxley declared:

Moralists of all ages and of all faiths, attending only to the relations of men towards one another in an ideal society, have agreed upon the 'golden rule', 'Do as you would be done by.' In other words, let sympathy be your guide; put yourself in the place of the man towards whom your action is directed; and do to him what you would like to have done to yourself under the circumstances.[6]

The present writer would not go so far, but would agree that the Golden Rule is found in the literature of most of the major living faiths in the world today as well as in the form of sayings that may be connected with at least some traditional religions associated with small-scale societies; some of these sayings have been put into writing. Also, as we shall see in the next chapter, even in traditional societies that may not possess Golden Rule sayings or proverbs, the principle of reciprocity is practised in connection with religious beliefs. In fact, it seems true that in all societies reciprocity is practised in some form, as it is so very fundamental in human relationships. To illustrate:

Now since the mother–child relation is the original unit of personal existence, the motivation of the child's behavior must be reciprocal, even if this reciprocity is, to begin with, merely implicit. The positive and negative poles of the infant's motivation are the germinal forms of love and fear respectively. . . This bipolar, reciprocal, love and fear motivation is concerned with maintaining the personal relationship in a common life between mother and child . . . The mother not only does what is needful for the child; she fondles him, caresses him, rocks him in her arms, and croons to him; and the baby responds with expressions of delight in his mother's care which have no biological significance. These gestures symbolize a mutual delight in the relation which unites them to a common life: they are expressions of affection through which each communicates to the other their delight in the relationship, and they represent, for its own sake, a consciousness of communicating.[7]

Our problem is that, although reciprocity is fundamental to human relationships and apparently is practised in all societies, it is impossible at present to prove that the Golden Rule in the form of written or unwritten sayings is found in connection with *every* existing religion, if under religion we rightly include the perhaps thousands of persuasions existing in small-scale societies in various parts of the world. Yet at the same time it is demonstrated in the following chapters that the Rule is found in even *more* religions and societies than has been commonly realised.

We do know, however, that the historical roots of the Golden Rule go far back into man's dim past. No one knows when or where it originated. Did some revelator whose name has been long forgotten first teach a small, prehistoric community an approximation to the Golden Rule? Did others, at later times and to different peoples, do the same? What was the role of seers and wise men (and women) in the process? At any rate, we do know that it must have been handed down generation after generation in some societies through word of mouth until finally put into writing – as happened, for instance, in Hinduism. (Brahmins memorised sacred teachings and passed them on orally for many hundreds of years before they were written.) We also know that there have been *so many* recorded statements of the Golden Rule throughout history that there is no possibility of compiling them all. No claim is made that the exposition in this book of such statements from the world's religions and other sources is exhaustive.

The question of *why* the Rule has been so widespread among so many peoples and religions and has been enunciated by so many philosophers and sages cannot be easily answered in these pages. No one has ever arrived at a satisfactory answer. But an attempt will be made in the last chapter.

The following chapters explore the boundless worlds of the Golden Rule as found in traditional religions, Hinduism, Jainism, Buddhism, Taoism, Confucianism, Zoroastrianism, Judaism, Christianity, Islám, Sikhism and the Bahá'í Faith – and introduce the possibility of its role in the future development of religion.

4

The Golden Rule in Traditional Religions and Societies

Traditional religions, frequently associated with small-scale societies, are found in all continents and are very numerous. Having lived in Africa for fifteen years, the present writer was naturally interested in general ethics and morals as well as particular Golden Rule statements found in African traditional religions. In black Africa,

. . . the morality of the societies . . . unquestionably rests on the ascendancy of custom and tradition, a set of predominantly peasant and family values and ideal images, an assured regularity born of recurring processes. Here it is a question of traditional morality, a product more collective than personal, which is strongly normative, founded on rules, duty, and law, a social structure which, although not always appearing authoritarian, nevertheless exercises a considerable diffuse pressure, especially by surrounding itself with a supernatural halo. It is a morality in which personal conscience and its aspirations certainly have a place, though a relatively reduced one. Prestigious and yet familiar models play a vital role: values do not have a characteristically abstract existence, but assume concrete incarnation in the persons of ancestors, chiefs, elders, and sages; in seers who are interpreters of the invisible, in devoted older sons, in obedient younger sons . . . It is the ideal of sociological interdependence which is going to prevail, expressing itself concretely through solidarity and a sense of responsibility towards one another.[1]

Interdependence, solidarity and reciprocity are characteristic of all these societies.

. . . The internal life of all the different groups – extended family as well as associations of equals – is governed by a law of interdependence and solidarity which places the common good above all other considerations, and demands that all bear the consequences of the possibly untoward conduct of one of the members . . . The help given to others is always free in the sense that no one expects any remuneration, but it is based on the principle of reciprocity . . .

The value of an individual [in Chad] is measured by his capacity to give his blood to a large number of descendants, food, lodging, and clothes to his neighbours and acquaintances, and to give gifts in return for those he has received.[2]

Moral norms have definitely been provided through the various traditional religions and are often affirmed and consolidated through periodical ceremonies. Although such generalisations as these about morals, ethics, and religion in African traditional societies may be stated, we should keep in mind that differences do exist. For instance, moral and social rules vary considerably from one ethnic group to another in black Africa, even among neighbouring populations.[3]

These have been primarily oral cultures; the word is absolutely essential in their pedagogy. Intellectual and ethical education is carried out not only through the life of the community as a whole but through fables, stories, myths, proverbs, maxims, riddles and songs.

In seeking examples of the Golden Rule in traditional religions and societies, the writer often turned to collections of proverbs – short sayings that usually point a moral or express an accepted truth based on human experience. But tracing the origins of most proverbs is an impossibility. Many must surely have a religious base, but others may not. The following, from Zanzibar, would not, we hope, have any religious origin:

Do harm to him who harms you; and fear him who harms you not.[4]

Of course, this saying cannot be termed an approximation of the Golden Rule, but it is nevertheless an example of the principle of reciprocity on a lower level.

Another example of a proverb that, in this instance, seems to correspond to 'eye for eye, tooth for tooth' reciprocity but can also be thought of on a higher level was provided by an African friend and is from the Kipsigis tribe of Kenya: 'If your sister cooks for you using a broken pot, do the same for her.' Kipsigis people understand this proverb to mean that if you do something bad to somebody the same will be done to you, so do what you want others to do for you.[5] An African scholar kindly provided a saying well known among the Kikuyu people of Kenya: 'Don't do evil to others, for if you do, you will pay for it here on earth.'[6]

Folktales have also been important in building ethical concepts in traditional societies. Interestingly, it has been discovered that variants of the same story are told in widely separate parts of the world. Again, it is often difficult to pinpoint whether a given folktale has a religious origin. At least two folktales illustrating 'eye for eye, tooth for tooth' reciprocity are to be found among the Kikuyu. One is summarised thus:

There is the story of how an unborn child avenged the death of its mother. The husband sees [a fruit] tree, tells his wife, who is expecting, to go up the tree and collect the fruit. She refuses. He climbs the tree and collects it. The woman gathers the fruit for him. He complains that she has eaten some and kills her. The child in the womb comes out and declares the murder to the in-laws. The man is killed in turn.[7]

Such stories are not confined to Africa. A folktale that was collected by Grimm and has been widespread throughout parts of Europe and Latin America tells how a man runs over a dog who is the friend of a sparrow. The sparrow takes vengeance. The man loses his horse, his property and finally his life.[8]

We should keep in mind, however, that although examples of 'eye for eye, tooth for tooth' reciprocity are to be found in proverbs and folktales in traditional societies, the vast majority of proverbs and folktales have dealt with other subjects.

The writer was delighted to find that Golden Rule approximations do exist among the Yoruba of West Africa, yet he was unable to find their equivalent in many other African traditional religions, or, even with the help of some friends, among the native Americans of North America, although his search was far from exhaustive. But it led him to question the claimed universality of the Golden Rule among the world's religions. Nor was he able to find any statement of the principle in the ancient national religion of Japan, Shinto, although it could possibly exist there.

An African scholar explained how important the Golden Rule has been to the Yoruba:

Yoruba ethics sums up what man-to-man relations should be in this: . . .
> Whenever a person breaks a stick in the forest,
> Let him consider what it would feel like if it were himself
>   (that was thus broken).

And . . .
> As sensitive to pain as are rats' little ones,
> So sensitive to pain are birds' little ones.

All these approximate to what has been described as the 'Golden Rule' – 'Do unto others as ye would that they should do unto you.' Yoruba elders teach that if everyone would first think in this way before acting, there would be perfectly good relations and happiness.[9]

The principle of universal unrequiting goodness or what some thinkers would term the 'Rule of Love' (see p. 64), is also to be found in African traditional religions. The following moving, poignant prayer of a dying man is to be found among the Dinka of the Sudan:

> And though I behold a man hate me,
> I will love him.
> O God, Father, help me, Father!
> O God, Creator, help me, Father!
> And even though I behold a man hate me,
> I will love him.[10]

We shall continue to discuss the issue of levels of reciprocity, as linked to the Golden Rule, in later chapters. However, there is evidence of the practice of reciprocity in traditional religions even when no Golden Rule sayings or proverbs may be perceived. For our example we turn to yet another part of the world. One of the writer's postgraduate students, whose home is Papua New Guinea, knew of no Golden Rule sayings as such among the indigenous people there but did provide a very interesting explanation of how religion and the practice of reciprocity are inseparable among various ethnic groups in that part of the world.

Hiri, Kula and *Tei* are well-known institutions of religious, social, economic and political significance in Papua New Guinea. Firstly, many weeks are devoted to spiritual preparation through fasting as well as material preparation. Everyone in the tribe(s), men and women, help in the preparation. But it is only men who make the long journeys, by sea (*Hiri* and *Kula*) and by land (*Tei*).

In the *Hiri* and *Kula* systems, a traditional pattern of trade was established many years ago. The participants travel in large outriggered canoes sailing over the seas for hundreds of kilometres to the receiving tribes' territories. After six to eight month intervals it is the receiving tribes' turns to make the journeys to reciprocate.

In the *Tei* system there is also a pattern that has been developed over many years. The participants walk many hundreds of kilometres to meet the opposite tribe(s) or clan(s). They are reciprocating what has been done to them by their hosts.

The principal aim of these institutions is to reciprocate. Among the participants various terms such as 'paying back', 'cementing friendship', 'bridging', and 'renewing comradeship' are used to underline the belief in reciprocity. Material things exchanged include a lot of food (pigs, sweet potatoes, fish, etc.), manufactured goods (clay pots, canoes, string bags, spears, etc.) and token payments (shell money, pigs' teeth, bird of paradise plumes, etc.). But *Tei* involves a 'cold war' between tribes that are rivals. The aim of reciprocity exists, but in practice it is a competition between two groups. Whichever appears as a winner is the one that brought more food and wealth to give to their rivals! In *Hiri* and *Kula*, on the other hand, the notion of reciprocity is strong and links with the strict rules about recognising all participants as equals. It is more a 'cementing', 'bridging', 'renewing' of friendships. During *Hiri* and *Kula* festivals, many different types of food and items of wealth are exchanged between the participants. If I give something to a particular friend from another tribe or clan, he will give my clan or family something of similar value in return next time.

Underlying all these activities is one thing that is religiously significant. Deep inside (the spirits) of the participants is the notion that the spirit of the clan or the tribe will travel with and guide them before, during, and after the planned journeys and will ensure the subsequent success of these activities. Throughout the whole process the spirits of ancestors are evoked and appeased. Spiritual and magical recitals are held throughout.[11]

Thus, it is clear that traditional religions and societies throughout the world make a significant contribution to our understanding and appreciation of the fundamental

importance of reciprocity in human relationships, of the
Iron Rule of 'eye for eye, tooth for tooth', of the Golden
Rule and of the Rule of Love.

5

In Hinduism

Hinduism is one of the world's great revealed religions and has its origins in remote antiquity. The vast majority of Hindus live in the Indian subcontinent; *Hindu* is a Persian word meaning 'Indian'. It was the term used by the Muslim Arabs of the eighth century AD to describe those people who lived beyond the Sind or Indus valley.[1] *Hinduism*, then, has become a Western term used by modern Hindus merely as a convenience when speaking or writing in English.

Hinduism is a vast and almost unbelievably intricate religion; in fact, it is regarded by some as a huge complex of religions rather than one religion. Scholars disagree on the few characteristics that virtually all Hindus have in common, one candidate being adherence to the caste system, another being belief in reincarnation. But many Hindus call their religion the *sanātana dharma*, 'eternal dharma' or 'eternal religion'. *Dharma* is a fundamental but extremely complex and subtle concept in Hinduism and may be understood in many different ways. *Dharma* is the most important and omnipresent word in the sacred Hindu texts, but these texts warn over and over again that this *dharma* is 'subtle' and 'very difficult to know'.[2] A Western scholar explained:

The word *dharma* is used in two distinct general senses in the great Hindu texts. It means first what is set down in the sacred texts themselves, and particularly in the texts dealing with Hindu customary law. In this usage it corresponds approximately to what we call 'canon law', a 'law' that is clearly defined, refined, and ever more minutely explained in the legal treatises themselves. By extension it is used to represent the religious assumptions on which these laws are based. *Dharma* in this sense is not at all 'difficult to know', for it is formulated at enormous length throughout the huge corpus of Hindu sacred literature, and is therefore, in its broadest connotation, best translated as 'religion'. [A closely related translation is 'a binding force'.] It is, then, both 'law' and 'religion'.

'Law' and 'religion' are, however, only expressions of something far more fundamental, and that is the eternal law that governs all human and non-human existence, what we would understand by 'natural law': and it is this law that is 'subtle' and almost impossible to know. In the natural order there is no difficulty, for it means no more than the laws that operate in nature and are nowadays the subject-matter of the natural sciences. But how do things stand in the moral order?[3]

The 'attitude of *dharma* is . . . concern for others as a fundamental extension of oneself'.[4]

From one point of view, ethics in the Hindu faith is closely related to the historical development of the social system in India. A fourfold division of society arose that seems to have been based on the actual division of labour in society in ancient India. This developed into a stratified social system that has been upheld for nearly 3,000 years. Full religious sanction has been given to the four classes (*varna*) and the many castes (*jati*). The four classes include those regarded as being learned in divine knowledge (*Brahman*), the warriors (*Kshatriya*), the merchants and craftsmen (*Vaishya*), and the menials (*Shudra*). Hindus have believed that this fourfold society is an essential part of the structure of the world; it must be preserved so that as many people as possible may gain salvation. But the system is weakening. A modern Hindu scholar explained:

the Gitā [*Bhagavad-Gitā*] declares that men fall into four classes because of their nature and actions (professions). Later on the four *Varṇas* became fixed by virtue of birth. Also many castes arose doubtless as occupational and functional groups to begin with, but later got stratified on [the] basis of birth. Now all castes practise all sorts of the professions and the original basis of the caste system is disappearing.[5]

Within each of the four classes there are not only very many castes but also clans or families (*kula*), and each of these units has its own set of duties imposed on it, which is called *dharma* – in this sense, its standard norm of conduct. However, the fact is that old practices have been called into question and new ones developed, especially in the twentieth century.

Also, Hindu ethics are linked to the cyclic Hindu view of *saṃsāra* – birth, death and rebirth – and *karma*, whereby the nature of a person's life is determined by his actions in a previous life, a concept based on interpretations of certain scriptural verses. Thus, for example, a person's status as a *Shudra* would have been determined by his actions in a life before this one. The ultimate aim is to escape *saṃsāra* and attain salvation.

Hindu ethics aim not only at the preservation of the social order but at the preservation of the family as well. The present writer's direct relationship with many people of Hindu background has revealed to him many examples of strong ethical practices associated with the family – for instance, the great respect shown for elder members of the family. For most Hindus today it would be unthinkable to place the grandparents of the family in 'old people's homes' as is done in the West; they are to be cared for lovingly within the family until death.

The Hindu texts contain many references to personal ethics, and much sacred literature of high ethical value exists. Very many Hindus revere the great figure of

Krishna, and the exquisitely beautiful and profound book associated with him, the *Bhagavad-Gītā* or 'Song of the Lord', which is found in the middle of the great Hindu epic the *Mahābhārata*, is generally regarded as one of the greatest and most influential of the Hindu sacred scriptures. The reader can be profoundly moved by the spiritual depths he discovers while reading the *Bhagavad-Gītā*.

The *Bhagavad-Gītā* may have been composed shortly before the Christian era, although its origins are more ancient.* At the very centre of the teachings of this great holy book are those about God. God, being the Creator of all things and working within them, is the source of both good and evil.[6] The struggle of good and evil in the soul of man is a central theme of the book.

The Golden Rule is found in the *Mahābhārata*, a vast and most important work, the longest epic in the world. The estimated dates of its composition range from the fourth century BC to the fourth century AD.[7] In it we find this approximation of the Golden Rule:

> Do not to others what ye do not wish
> Done to yourself; and wish for others too
> – What ye desire and long for, for yourself
> – This is the whole of Ḍharma, heed it well.[8]

As we shall see over and over again with the great faiths of the world, there is more than one Golden Rule statement associated with Hinduism, and this is one indication of how fundamental it is. About the fourth century AD a whole mass of sacred literature known as the *Purāṇas* was taking shape among the Hindus.[9] *Purāṇas* at one time were the medium for conveying Vedic teaching to unlettered people, including the lower castes and the majority of women.[10] From a purely religious point of view, by far the most important of the *Purāṇas* was the *Bhāgavata Purāṇa*,

---

* Some scholars do not accept these estimated dates.

compiled probably in the ninth century AD.[11] Krishna is the central figure in the *Bhāgavata Purāṇa*. Here again we find the Golden Rule and its link with that most fundamental word, *dharma*:

> This Dharma stands unchallenged changelessly,
> That I should sorrow when my fellow-beings
> May sorrow, and rejoice when they rejoice.[12]

The *Manu-smṛti* (the Code or Institutes of Manu) is a collection of laws based on custom and precedent and the teaching of the Vedas.[13] '. . . The Code of Manu is accepted by most branches of Hinduism as the most complete expression of Hindu law.'[14] This very important work is traditionally attributed to the first Manu, Svāyambhuva ('the Self-existent'). In it divine revelation (*śruti*) and empirical knowledge (*smṛti*) (another translation is 'code of Hindu law delivered originally by tradition') are drawn upon to define the Law of Conduct and to apply it, though not always impartially, to all classes of the community.[15] 'Manu is said to have learnt the "Institutes" from the Creator himself, and in turn transmitted them to the first ten sages; finally entrusting Bhṛgu with its exposition . . .'[16] (The claim of transmission of the law directly from the Creator is paralleled, as we shall note again later, in the Mosaic law and other instances.) In the *Manu-smṛti* we find these words:

> Who sees Me in all beings, and all in Me,
> He sacrifices unto Me in all;
> His life is all one constant 'sacri-fice',
> 'Good-act'; he only gains the true Svā-rājya,
> 'Reign of the Higher Self', Kingdom of Heaven.
> Who looks at others' wives as on his mothers,
> Who looks at others' gold as so much dross,
> Who feels for others *as he feels for self*,
> He is [a] true pandit, he is [a] true wise man.[17]

The *Hitopadeśa* (friendly advice, salutary instruction) is a well-known collection of ethical tales and fables. Many translations of the *Hitopadeśa* have been adapted to the religious and social ideas of different peoples.[18] Again an approximation of the Golden Rule is found therein:

> The final mark of Duty, Righteousness,
> Legal and moral Lawfulness, is this –
> That what ye hold *as dear and good for self*
> And which your inner higher self approves,
> Ye hold as dear and good for others too;
> And what ye may not like for your own self,
> For others like it not, in the same way,
> Who *feeleth as his own* the joys and sorrows
> Of others, he is the true yogī, he
> Hath truly 'joined' his own soul with all souls.[19]

We should note in the last few lines of this fine statement an evident 'concern for others as a fundamental extension of oneself'. We may very well, to some extent, feel as our own the joys and sorrows of others. Many of us have had such experiences. But how far one soul may go in 'joining' with 'all souls' in following the Golden Rule is a difficult question indeed – as we shall see further in our investigation of Jainism, Buddhism, Taoism, and Zoroastrianism.

What strikes the reader of Golden Rule statements in the Hindu faith is how absolutely *fundamental* they are. We find:

> This is the whole of Ḍharma, heed it well.

> This Ḍharma stands unchallenged changelessly.

> He is [a] true pandit, he is [a] true wise man.

> The final mark of Duty, Righteousness,
> Legal and moral Lawfulness, is this

And we shall discover over and over again in the following chapters the fundamental importance of the Golden Rule in the religions of the world.

6

In Jainism

Like Hinduism, Jainism is regarded as an ancient religion of India, and most of its present-day followers live in that land. Jainism developed originally partly as a reaction to certain objectionable principles and practices in ancient Brahmanism such as bloody animal sacrifices; thus it may also be regarded as an ancient reform movement. Some authorities maintain that Jainism is a sect of Hinduism, while others state it is a religion in its own right. A Jain scholar explained, ' . . . Jainism is not a revealed religion and claims no divine origin.'[1] Jainism has many links with both Hinduism and Buddhism.

The Jainas maintain that theirs is a very ancient system going much further back in antiquity than the time of its most prominent and respected figure, Vardhamāna Mahāvīra (599–527 BC). A historian of world religions explained:

[Jainism's] fundamental viewpoint is that the whole universe is animated by countless individual souls; not only human beings but all living things are believed to be inhabited by souls. This applies to animals, insects and even plants. Each of these souls may be said to inhabit a material body, but more precisely this is an imprisonment from which the soul seeks to escape. It was in this view of existence and in the method of escape taught by the Mahāvīra that his doctrine differed from both Brahmanism and Buddhism.[2]

In this connection, Jainism is also noted for the subtle and complex principle of *ahiṁsā* (non-violence, non-killing, non-injury, non-hatred, harmlessness, etc.), a principle that forms the moral basis of the entire Jain discipline.

In the system of Jain ethics it [non-violence] constitutes the first of the moral vows. Jain ethics can be said to be built on non-violence, because all other moral virtues are included as specific aspects of non-violence.[3]

The Jain aims not to harm or, especially, kill anything. *Hiṁsā* (harm, hurt, killing, robbery) is the worst of the eighteen chief sins.[4] Jainas believe that '. . . the current of life in the lowliest insect is as sacred as in the most noble and exalted of human beings, and is as eternal'.[5] Jain monks are forbidden to take life at any level, and Jainas generally avoid following occupations that could cause destruction of life, such as farming, which involves killing small creatures when tilling the soil.

In Jainism, three ideals, the *triratna* or 'three jewels', are upheld: *Samyag-Darsha* or right faith, *Samyag-Jyana* or right knowledge, and *Samyag-Charitra* or right conduct. Jainism prescribes elaborate rules of everyday conduct.

The Jain scriptures were systematised and put into writing around AD 300–400. The eleven *Angas* make up the main part of the Jain sacred literature for the Svetāmbara sect, but there are other sacred books. Among the *Angas*, the *Āchāra-aṅga* gives a full exposition of the rules of conduct for the monks or ascetics.[6] The *Āchāra-aṅga* is among the oldest parts of the Āgamas (canons). The Āgamas themselves are said to be based on compilations from discourses of Mahāvīra by his direct disciples. In the *Āchāra-aṅga-sūtra* we find:

> Thus we enjoin on you, thus do we say,
> Thus we believe, thus we proclaim to all;
> No living things should be slain anywhere,

Nor ordered forcibly this way or that,
Nor put in bonds, nor tortured any way,
Or treated violently otherwise;
Because you are that same which ye would slay,
Or order here and there against his will,
Or put in prison, or subject to pain,
Or treat with violence; *ye are that same*;
The Self-same Life doth circulate in all.[7]

The same position is taken in the *Yoga-Śāstra*, a non-canonical work:

In happiness and suffering, in joy and grief, we should regard all creatures as we regard our own self, and should therefore refrain from inflicting upon others such injury as would appear undesirable to us if inflicted upon ourselves.[8]

To some, the Jain understanding of the Golden Rule as applying to *all living things* seems extreme. Thomas Henry Huxley, who was a well-known biologist and palaeontologist, voiced an objection to such a position that others may share: 'What would become of the garden if the gardener treated all the weeds and slugs and birds and trespassers as he would like to be treated, if he were in their place?'[9] Nevertheless, many admire the love and compassion Jainas demonstrate towards all living creatures. Jainas build asylums and rest houses for old and diseased animals where they are fed and kept until death comes to them naturally.

A moderate view of the treatment of other living things and a somewhat different rationale for kindness towards living creatures is found in the writings of the Bahá'í Faith, for example in these words of 'Abdu'l-Bahá:

Briefly, it is not only their fellow human beings that the beloved of God must treat with mercy and compassion, rather must they show forth the utmost loving-kindness to every living creature.

For in all physical respects, and where the animal spirit is concerned, the selfsame feelings are shared by animal and man. Man hath not grasped this truth, however, and he believeth that physical sensations are confined to human beings, wherefore is he unjust to the animals, and cruel.

And yet in truth, what difference is there when it cometh to physical sensations? The feelings are one and the same, whether ye inflict pain on man or on beast. There is no difference here whatever. And indeed ye do worse to harm an animal, for man hath a language, he can lodge a complaint, he can cry out and moan; if injured he can have recourse to the authorities and these will protect him from his aggressor. But the hapless beast is mute, able neither to express its hurt nor take its case to the authorities. If a man inflict a thousand ills upon a beast, it can neither ward him off with speech nor hale him into court. Therefore is it essential that ye show forth the utmost considera- tion to the animal, and that ye be even kinder to him than to your fellow man . . .

Most human beings are sinners, but the beasts are innocent. Surely those without sin should receive the most kindness and love – all except animals which are harmful, such as bloodthirsty wolves, such as poisonous snakes, and similar pernicious creatures, the reason being that kindness to these is an injustice to human beings and to other animals as well. If, for example, ye be tender-hearted toward a wolf, this is but tyranny to a sheep, for a wolf will destroy a whole flock of sheep.[10]

The foregoing discussion suggests that there may be four basic positions a person is likely to take when deciding towards whom he should practise the Golden Rule:

a. to apply it to all living things, including man, without exception,
b. to apply it to all living things, including man, with certain exceptions,
c. to apply it to all human beings only, excluding all other living things, and

   d. to apply it to some human beings only, excluding all
      other living things.

For a man consistently to apply the Golden Rule to living
things other than man but not to other human beings would
be most unusual!

7

In Buddhism

Another great faith emerged from the Indian subcontinent –
Buddhism. Gautama, later to be known by the religious
title of the Buddha (the Enlightened, or Awakened, One),
was born near the present-day border of India and Nepal in
563 BC and passed away in 483. Buddha was truly one of the
great figures in the history of the world's religions. He was
deeply concerned about suppressing the widespread pain
and suffering in the world. Although few Buddhists remain
in India, the faith has spread widely throughout many parts
of Asia, with a scattering of adherents in other continents as
well.

The Buddhist faith places great emphasis on a moral life.

The Buddhist way has three principal features: morality,
meditation and wisdom. Morality is the indispensable basis of the
system. The essence of Buddhist morality is contained in the five
precepts (pañcaśīlā): to abstain from taking life, from falsehood,
from taking what is not given (i.e. theft), from sexual miscon-
duct, and from using intoxicants and drugs, which tend to cloud
the mind. Upon the foundation of a serious resolve to keep these
precepts can then be built the practice of meditation, or concen-
tration (samādhi).[1]

However, a fundamental question arises among scholars as
to how much of Buddha's inspired, original teachings
survive in their pure form in modern Buddhism and how

much has been altered or lost. The identical question may
be asked regarding the teachings of other founders of the
world's religions.

Fundamental among the sacred scriptures of the
Buddhist faith is the *Tripitaka* (The Threefold Basket), so
called because it is divided into three 'baskets' (*pitaka*), or
collections of writings. The *Tripitaka*, which is preserved in
the Pali language, is also known as the Theravada canon.
The three 'baskets' include the *Vinaya Pitaka* (Discipline
Basket), which contains the rules of discipline of the order,
the *Sutta Pitaka* (Teaching Basket), consisting of the
discourses of the Buddha, and the *Abhidhamma Pitaka*
(Higher Doctrine or Metaphysical Basket), including
expositions of the intricate points of Buddhist psychology
and doctrine.[2]

The *Sutta Pitaka* (Teaching Basket) consists of five
Nikayas (collections). The *Dīgha-Nīkāya* is the division of
long discourses; in it is found the *Sigālovāda-sutta*, in which
Buddha is represented as finding the householder Sigala
worshipping the six quarters (east, west, south and north,
nadir and zenith). Buddha expounds the duties of a layman
by explaining this worship as fulfilling one's duties to six
classes of persons (parents, friends and companions, etc.).
Herein we find:

In five ways should a clansman minister to his friends and
familiars as the northern quarter – by generosity, courtesy, and
benevolence . . . by treating them as he treats himself, and by
being as good as his word.[3]

Another of the five Nikayas in the *Sutta Pitaka* is the
Majjhima-Nīkāya, the division of discourses of medium
length. Yet another approximation to the Golden Rule is
given in this work:

Is there a deed, Rahula, thou dost wish to do? Then bethink thee thus: 'Is this deed conducive to my own harm, or to others' harm, or to that of both?' Then is this a bad deed, entailing suffering. Such a deed must thou surely not do.[4]

The fifth of the Nikayas is the *Khuddaka-Nīkāya* (collection of the little texts), one of which is the famous work known as the *Dhamma-pada* (Sayings on Dharma or Words of the Doctrine) in the Pali canon and the *Udanavarga* in its Sanskrit version. We cite the version in the Pali canon:

> All shrink from suffering, and all love life;
> Remember that thou too art like to them;
> *Make thine own self the measure of the others,*
> And so abstain from causing hurt to them.[5]

The *Khuddaka-Nīkāya* also includes the *Jātaka*, verses belonging to 547 tales of previous existences of Buddha. In the *Mataka-bhaṭṭa Jātaka* we find:

> Who knoweth this great Truth – that Life is one
> In all, and how all pain originates,
> He hurteth not his one hand with his other,
> Knowing that he himself will suffer pain.[6]

Three of the citations above link the Golden Rule with man's experiences of suffering and pain, a central theme in the teachings of Buddha. The last one clearly relates to the rationale for following the Golden Rule quoted in Chapter 6 from the Jain *Āchāra-aṅga-sūtra*:

> *Because you are that same* which ye would slay,
> Or order here and there against his will,
> Or put in prison, or subject to pain,
> Or treat with violence; *ye are that same*;
> The Self-same Life doth circulate in all.

The connection between the two faiths in this respect is explained in some detail:

About 500 BC two religions came to the fore in India which placed 'No Harming' into the very centre of their doctrine – the one being Jainism and the other Buddhism. This special emphasis on the prohibition of doing harm to any living being was presumably a reaction against the increase in violence, which marked human relationships as a consequence of the invention of bronze and iron. It was directed in India not only against the massacres which marked tribal warfare, but also against the enormous slaughter of animals which accompanied the Vedic sacrifice, and to some extent against the cruelty which marks the attitude of peasants to animals. The doctrine of Jains and Buddhists is based on two principles:

1. The belief in the kinship of everything that lives, which is further strengthened by the doctrine of reincarnation, according to which the same being is to-day a man, tomorrow a rabbit, after that a moth, and then again a horse. By ill-treating an animal one might thus find oneself in the invidious position of ill-treating one's deceased mother or one's best friend.

2. The second principle is expressed in the Udana, where the Buddha says: *'My thought has wandered in all directions throughout the world. I have never yet met with anything that was dearer to anyone than his own self. Since to others, to each one for himself, the self is dear, therefore let him who desires his own advantage not harm another.'* In other words, we should cultivate our emotions so that we feel with others as if they were ourselves. If we allow the virtue of compassion to grow in us, it will not occur to us to harm anyone else, any more than we willingly harm ourselves. It will be seen that in this way we diminish our sentiment and love of self by widening the boundaries of what we regard as ours. By inviting, as it were, everybody's self to enter our own personality, we break down the barriers which separate us from others.

Through this attitude, Buddhism can be said to have had an immense humanising effect on the entire history of Asia. It is the kindness of everyone which strikes the observers in countries saturated by Buddhism, such as Burma.[7]

The immensely beneficial effect Buddhism has had on a large segment of the human race is undoubted, and the

Golden Rule teachings in its sacred scriptures have played their part in this process. Yet the nagging question still remains: do we possess the original Golden Rule and other teachings of that wonderful soul, Buddha, today? And do we possess the same for other founders of the world's great faiths?

In Chapters 5, 6 and 7 we have noted the fundamental importance of the Golden Rule in the three great faiths of Indian origin: Hinduism, Jainism, and Buddhism. As one scholar claims, 'It is the common ethical ideal in Indian thought.'[8]

8

In Taoism

Like Confucianism, Taoism originated in ancient China. The question has arisen whether originally Taoism was a religion at all, or just a philosophy.[1] One authority has declared that Taoism did not become organised as a religion until shortly before the Christian era.[2] Historically, however, Taoism has had a profound impact on morality in China. Religiously-inclined persons in China today often combine elements of Buddhism, Confucianism, and Taoism in their beliefs.

The real 'fathers of Taoism' were Lao-Tse, Lie-Tse and Kuang-Tse, the most prominent being the great and humble sage Lao-Tse. We know very little for certain about the life of Lao-Tse (604–517? BC). The only certain date is when he met Confucius in 518. In fact, so little is known that some scholars have doubted if he really was an historical figure at all.

Lao-Tse, Lie-Tse and Kuang-Tse did not so much promulgate new and challenging doctrines as develop elements of thought present in more primitive forms.[3] But Lao-Tse was one of the first religious teachers of the world to teach the principle of universal unrequiting goodness.[4]

The greatest literary masterpiece of Taoism, the *Tâo-Teh-King* (Canon of Reason and Virtue) is usually attributed to Lao-Tse. The *Tâo-Teh-King* is a much-appreciated and much-translated work. The ethical ideal inculcated in it is ' . . . a quiet, restful, simplicity, like that of Heaven itself'.[5] The principle of universal unrequiting goodness is clearly shown in the following approximation to the Golden Rule from the *Tâo-Teh-King*:

To those who are good (to me), I am good; and to those who are not good (to me), I am also good; – and thus (all) get to be good. To those who are sincere (with me), I am sincere; and to those who are not sincere (with me), I am also sincere; – and thus (all) get to be sincere.[6]

Again:

(It is the way of the Tâo) to act without (thinking of) acting; to conduct affairs without (feeling the) trouble of them; to taste without discerning any flavour; to consider what is small as great, and a few many; *and to recompense injury with kindness.*[7] (Author's italics.)

The principle of universal unrequiting goodness has been amply demonstrated in the lives and teachings of the founders of the great religions of the world such as Jesus Christ, Muḥammad and Bahá'u'lláh. Jesus Christ taught the principle as recorded in the Bible in Luke 6:27–36:*

But I say unto you which hear, Love your enemies, do good to them which hate you, bless them that curse you, and pray for them which despitefully use you. And unto him that smiteth thee on the *one* cheek offer also the other; and him that taketh away thy cloke forbid not *to take thy* coat also. Give to every man that asketh of thee; and of him that taketh away thy goods ask *them* not again. And as ye would that men should do to you, do ye also to them likewise. For if ye love them which love you, what thank have ye? for sinners also love those that love them. And if ye do good to them which do good to you, what thank have ye? for sinners also do even the same. And if ye lend *to them* of whom ye hope to receive, what thank have ye? for sinners also lend to sinners, to receive as much again. But love ye your enemies, and

* See also Matthew 5:38–48.

do good, and lend, hoping for nothing again; and your reward shall be great, and ye shall be the children of the Highest: for he is kind unto the unthankful and to the evil. Be ye therefore merciful, as your Father also is merciful.

And he exemplified this great principle when, after having been betrayed by Judas Iscariot, having been taken before Pontius Pilate, having been sentenced to death by him after repeated demands from the hostile crowd, and having been ignominiously led to his place of execution, he said at that fateful spot (Luke 23:34), 'Father, forgive them; for they know not what they do.' These very words were cried out by Bahá'ís of Yazd, Persia, in the early years of the twentieth century as they were dying as martyrs at the hands of their executioners: 'O Lord! forgive them; they know not what they do.'[8]

Another memorable story illustrating universal unrequiting goodness is found in the life of Muḥammad, an exemplary life replete with suffering:

He was stern in punishing criminals, but always forgave personal enemies; for example Habrar, who drove the end of his lance against the Prophet's daughter, as she was mounting her camel to flee from Mecca. She was far advanced in pregnancy; she fell to the ground, and later died from the injury. Habrar threw himself on Muhammad's mercy, and was pardoned.[9]

But the principle has been lived by some of the greatest followers of the world's religions as well. One of the most impressive illustrations is found in a story about 'Abdu'l-Bahá, the son of Bahá'u'lláh, who with his illustrious father and others had been forced into exile and imprisonment for many years because of his religious beliefs. Bahá'ís believe 'Abdu'l-Bahá was the exemplar of every Bahá'í ideal and virtue. The setting of the story is in the foul prison-city of 'Akká, in the Holy Land, around AD 1870–90:

When the Master ['Abdu'l-Bahá] came to Akka there lived there a certain man [Ḥáji Ṣiddíq] from Afghanistan, an austere and rigid Mussulman [Muslim]. To him the Master was a heretic. He felt and nourished a great enmity towards the Master, and roused up others against him. When opportunity offered in gatherings of the people, as in the Mosque, he denounced him with bitter words.

'This man', he said to all, 'is an imposter. Why do you speak to him? Why do you have dealings with him?' And when he passed the Master on the street he was careful to hold his robe before his face that his sight might not be defiled.

Thus did the Afghan. The Master, however, did thus: The Afghan was poor and lived in a mosque; he was frequently in need of food and clothing. The Master sent him both. These he accepted, but without thanks. He fell sick. The Master took him a physician, food, medicine, money. These, also, he accepted; but as he held out one hand that the physician might take his pulse, with the other he held his cloak before his face that he might not look upon the Master. *For twenty-four years* the Master continued his kindnesses and the Afghan persisted in his enmity. Then at last one day the Afghan came to the Master's door, and fell down, penitent and weeping, at his feet.

'Forgive me, sir!' he cried. 'For twenty-four years I have done evil to you, for twenty-four years you have done good to me. Now I know that I have been in the wrong.'

The Master bade him arise, and they became friends.

This Master is as simple as his soul is great. He claims nothing for himself – neither comfort, nor honour, nor repose. Three or four hours of sleep suffice him; all the remainder of his time and all his strength are given to the succour of those who suffer, in spirit or in body. 'I am', he says, 'the servant of God.'[10]

Thus, Christianity, Islám, and the Bahá'í Faith provide us with excellent illustrations, in one sense or another, of Lao-Tse's maxim:

To those who are good (to me), I am good; and to those who are not good (to me), I am also good; – and thus (all) get to be good.

And

. . . Recompense injury with kindness.

The *T'ai Shang Kan Ying P'ien* (Tractate of Actions and Their Retributions) is another, much later, Taoist scripture. 'This is highly esteemed by the Taoists themselves and also by students of the world's living religions for the reach of its ethical ideals.'[11] Herein we find:

Pity the misfortunes of others; rejoice in the well-being of others; help those who are in want; save men in danger; rejoice at the success of others; and sympathise with their reverses, *even as though you were in their place.*[12]

The reader will note the difference between conducting oneself according to the Golden Rule through *thinking of oneself as being in the place of others* as in this Taoist statement and conducting oneself in conformity with the Golden Rule *because you think you are one with other living things* as given in certain statements in previous chapters.

Another fine Golden Rule statement from the *T'ai Shang Kan Ying P'ien* reads:

Regard your neighbour's gain as your own gain: regard your neighbour's loss as your own loss.[13]

Thus, Taoism provides us with its share of gems in our search through the boundless worlds of the Golden Rule.

9

In Confucianism

Authorities generally agree that K'ung-fu-tse (551–479 BC), known in the West as Confucius, was not a prophet; some feel that he was not even a philosopher. This great man of China has been called a sage, the founder of a moral system, a great reformer, or simply a gentleman who had a fine sense of what is done and what is not done. Some authorities therefore claim that Confucianism is not a religion but an ethic, but others argue that it has the characteristics of a religion.

It must be emphasized that 'Confucianism' was so named by Westerners who supposed that it was a religion founded by Confucius, as Christianity was founded by Christ and Muhammadanism [sic] by Muhammad. But when 'Confucians' wish to distinguish themselves, they do not call themselves after their supposed founder, but by a word of uncertain origin, *ju*; and they speak of their principles by such phrases as 'the way of the sages', 'the way of the ancients'. This 'Way' (Tao), which is first of all a system of government and of rules of behaviour for members of the governing class, is assumed to have existed from time immemorial.[1]

The ethics of Confucianism centres on the fundamental principle of social propriety.

The comparative statement might almost be made that in no other religious group has there been such actual insistence upon

the principle of every individual performing properly his several
and reciprocal social duties.[2]

The ethical ideal for the individual is embodied in the
'superior man', who is often contrasted with the 'mean
man'. K'ung-fu-tse's reform of the ethical basis of society
was supported by him through reference to the example of
the ancients.

The books of Confucianism were, for a long period of
time, the basis of China's orthodox philosophy and the
guide to ethics and morals. When classifying the Confucian
books a distinction is made between the books that K'ung-
fu-tse edited and, to a small degree, wrote, and those that
were written later in the spirit of his teaching.[3] Those in the
first category are termed Wu-ching ('five canonical books')
and in the second Sze-shu ('four classical books'). The five
canonical books include:

1. The *Shu-ching* (*Book of Documents*).
2. The *Shi-ching* (*Book of Songs*).
3. The *Li-chi* (*Notes on Manners*), a compendium of
   proprieties.
4. The *Ki-King* (*Book of Changes*).
5. The *Ch'un Ch'iu* (*Spring and Autumn Annals of the
   State of Lu*), the only work that was unquestionably
   written by K'ung-fu-tse himself.

The four classical post-Confucian books (*Sze-shu*),
which were either written about him personally or about
his doctrines by various followers, include:

1. *Analects of Confucius* (*Lun Yu*), collected sayings of
   Confucius.
2. *The Great Learning* (*Ta-hio*), teachings concerning
   virtues.
3. *The Doctrine of the Mean* (*Chung Yung*), perfect
   moderation.
4. The work of Meng-tzŭ (Mencius, *c* 372–238 BC).

No theological doctrine of inspiration or supernatural authority has ever been developed concerning the books of Confucianism.

It must be stressed that the principle of reciprocal propriety is absolutely fundamental in Confucianism, and this has a direct connection with the Golden Rule. The *Analects of Confucius* is regarded as the most direct source for the doctrines of K'ung-fu-tse. In it conversations take place, chiefly between the great sage and his disciples. Herein we find the following fundamental statement:

Tsze-kung asked, saying, 'Is there one word which may serve as a rule of practice for all one's life?' The Master said, 'Is not RECIPROCITY such a word? What you do not want done to yourself, do not do to others.'[4]

The principle of reciprocal propriety is to be applied especially in the Five Relationships. (The code of the five social relations was developed by later Confucianists.)[5]

There are the relations of ruler and subject, father and son, husband and wife, elder brother and younger, friend and friend . . . No one, intelligent or stupid, can dispense with these for a single day.[6]

K'ung-fu-tse probably said more about the relationship between ruler and subject than the others, but among the Chinese people over the centuries the filial relationship, which was the basis of the strong family system in that land, has been paramount.

The principle of reciprocal propriety, then, is to be applied to a wide variety of people. The broad applicability of the principle is further illustrated in *The Great Learning*, a book in which teachings about virtue are given.

What the Great Learning teaches, is to illustrate illustrious virtue; to love the people; and to rest in the highest excellence . . .

What a man dislikes in his superiors, let him not display in his

treatment of his inferiors; and what he dislikes in his inferiors, let
him not display in his service of his superiors; what he dislikes in
those who are before him, let him not therewith precede those
who are behind him; and what he dislikes in those who are behind
him, let him not therewith follow those who are before him;
what he dislikes to receive on the right, let him not bestow on the
left; and what he dislikes to receive on the left, let him not bestow
on the right: – this is what is called 'The Principle with which, as
with a measuring square, to regulate one's course.'[7]

The twelfth chapter of *The Doctrine of the Mean* contains
the words of Tsze-sze and is designed to illustrate what is
said in the first chapter, that 'The path may not be left'. In
the thirteenth chapter he quotes the words of K'ung-fu-tse
to further illustrate this. Again, stress is placed on the
fundamental principle of reciprocity, but K'ung-fu-tse
admits that he personally is unable to live up to it in practice.
In fact, the sage admits elsewhere as well that he suffered
from moral shortcomings but hoped for improvement. For
this we should laud him. Such an honest assessment of
oneself and a steadfast will to improve is a healthy sign that
one is on the path of moral development.

The Master said, 'The path is not far from man. When men try to
pursue a course, which is far from the common indications of
consciousness, this course cannot be considered THE PATH . . .
    When one cultivates to the utmost the principles of his nature,
and exercises them on the principle of reciprocity, he is not far
from the path. What you do not like when done to yourself, do
not do to others.
    In the way of the superior man there are four things, to not one
of which have I as yet attained. – To serve my father, as I would
require my son to serve me: to this I have not attained; to serve
my prince, as I would require my minister to serve me: to this I
have not attained; to serve my elder brother, as I would require
my younger brother to serve me: to this I have not attained; to set
the example in behaving to a friend, as I would require him to

behave to me: to this I have not attained. Earnest in practising the ordinary virtues, and careful in speaking about them, if, in his practice, he has anything defective, the superior man dares not but exert himself; and if, in his words, he has any excess, he dares not allow himself such licence. Thus his words have respect to his actions, and his actions have respect to his words; is it not just an entire sincerity which marks the superior man?'[8]

This honest assessment of one's shortcomings yet determination to strive to practise the Golden Rule, is also demonstrated in the *Analects of Confucius* by one of K'ung-fu-tse's disciples:

Chung-kung asked about perfect virtue. The Master said, '*It is*, when you go abroad, *to behave to every one* as if you were receiving a great guest; to employ the people as if you were assisting at a great sacrifice; not to do to others as you would not wish done to yourself; to have no murmuring against you in the country, and none in the family.' Chung-kung said, 'Though I am deficient in intelligence and vigour, I will make it my business to practise this lesson.'[9]

Some men profess to be virtuous and may even claim to be practising the Golden Rule in their lives, yet the facts do not match their claims. K'ung-fu-tse, being a keen observer of human nature, observed this fault in the character of others. For instance, Book V of the *Analects of Confucius* is chiefly occupied with the judgement of the sage on the character of several of his disciples and other persons. In it we read:

Tsze-kung said, 'What I do not wish men to do to me, I also wish not to do to men.' The Master said, 'Ts'ze, you have not attained to that.'[10]

Hopefully, Tsze-kung's shortcoming in this respect was not extreme. But the world today is sadly full of people whose words do not match their deeds and inner thoughts.

Hypocrisy is rampant. We need not merely dwell on the faults of others in this respect; we can start by taking an honest look within ourselves.

The devastatingly tragic effects of hypocrisy are exemplified in the story of Judas Iscariot, the treacherous disciple of Jesus Christ. It was he whose evil intent – which was known to Jesus but hidden from others – led to the execution of Jesus. In Matthew 26:14–16, 47–50 we find:

Then one of the twelve, called Judas Iscariot, went unto the chief priests. And said *unto them*, What will ye give me, and I will deliver him unto you? And they covenanted with him for thirty pieces of silver. And from that time he sought opportunity to betray him . . .

Judas . . . came, and with him a great multitude with swords and staves, from the chief priests and elders of the people. Now he that betrayed him gave them a sign, saying, Whomsoever I shall kiss, that same is he: hold him fast. And forthwith he came to Jesus, and said, Hail, master; and kissed him. And Jesus said unto him, Friend, wherefore art thou come? Then came they, and laid hands on Jesus, and took him.

Few today may possess the extreme degree of hypocrisy of a Judas, but how often, in one form or another, the insincere pretend false affection for others! How many are those who falsely profess peace, who falsely profess unity, love, fellowship, the Golden Rule!

The great religious figures, philosophers and sages in human history who have set forth the Golden Rule in one form or another have had a profound effect on their followers and those who admired them and their teachings. These 'moons' reflecting the light of the 'suns' have usually attempted to understand the teachings more deeply and to try to find ways and means of applying them effectively in their own and others' lives. This has involved the process of interpretation.

Perhaps the greatest philosopher in China to be influenced by K'ung-fu-tse was Meng Tzǔ (Master Meng), or Mencius (the Latinised form of the name). Meng Tzǔ came to be recognised in China as a sage second only to K'ung-fu-tse. After Meng Tzǔ's death, his disciples put together his teachings in the *Book of Mencius*. His work is considered to be the best interpretation of the ideas of K'ung-fu-tse; he exerted an immense influence and made a decisive contribution to the victory of Confucianism in China. Meng Tzǔ declared,

If one strives to treat others as he would be treated by them he will come near the perfect life.[11]

Another prominent Chinese philosopher who was greatly influenced by the teachings of K'ung-fu-tse was Wang Yang-ming (AD 1472–1529). In one of his philosophical letters addressed to Huang Tsung-hsien, he expounded briefly on the central principle of reciprocity in Confucianism as stated in *Analects of Confucius*, 5:11:

What men do to me, that I do not wish, I do not do to them. What I do wish, proceeds from the desire of my heart, naturally and spontaneously, without being forced. Not doing to others [what they do not wish] is possible after some effort. This indicates the difference between *jen* [humanity] and *shu* [reciprocity].* But reciprocity, the method of acquiring humanity, is precisely our business.[12]

The process of the influence of Golden Rule statements upon subsequent formulations of the same principle is a complex one, as we shall see again in later chapters.

---

* *Jen* may also be translated as love, magnanimity, etc., and is regarded as the key concept in Confucian moral philosophy, with *shu* being a derivative of *jen*. See Yi-Pao Mei, 'Moral Philosophies of China', pp. 75–6.

10

In Zoroastrianism

One of the truly extraordinary figures in the history of religion was the prophet Zarathustra. Scholars disagree widely about the dates of his life – ranging from 6000 BC to 1400 BC to 1000 BC to the seventh or sixth century BC. Zarathustra's homeland was possibly in eastern Iran: 'Zarathustra' is the Old Iranian form of his name, but he is also known as Zoroaster, which is the Greek form. 'Zarathustra belongs in the category of prophet, in that he appears to have undergone religious experiences which led him to proclaim certain truths which had been disclosed to him about the nature of the spiritual world.'[1] He is said to have written very profusely.

Most followers of the Zoroastrian faith today live in India, specifically the Bombay area, with a smaller number in Iran and other countries. Zoroastrianism is known in India as the religion of the Parsis. It has had an important impact on other faiths, particularly Judaism and Christianity.

Scholars often maintain that in its original stage, as promulgated by Zarathustra himself, Zoroastrianism was fundamentally a monotheistic religion. But the prophet's original teachings were often altered over the years. The next stage was the Zoroastrianism of the Persian Empire when elements were introduced that greatly tempered its monotheistic nature. Third was a renewal of the religion during the time of the Arsacid and Sassanian dynasties (AD 226–642), and finally there is the relatively modern period.

Zarathustra taught of the existence and nature of one God, Ahura Mazdā, the 'Wise Lord'. There is, as some scholars put it, a 'dualism' that is linked with the monotheism of the Zoroastrian faith. '[This] was a dualism of spirit, postulating two principles at the origin of the Universe – the Spirit of Good or Ohrmazd, and the Spirit of Evil or Ahriman.'[2]

According to some Zoroastrians:

Zarathustra represented these two opposed spirits as twins, one of whom chose good, while the other chose evil. He seems to have regarded the twin cosmic principles as having had their origin in the one supreme Wise Lord, Ahura Mazdā. They are designated in the Zoroastrian scriptures by the names *Spenta Mainyu* (Holy Spirit) and *Angra Mainyu* (Evil Spirit). The relationship of the former to Ahura Mazdā was obviously closer than was that of the latter. It is for this reason that in later tradition the Holy Spirit comes to be identified with Ahura Mazdā (or in the alternative form Ohrmazd).[3]

But the doctrine of the two co-eternal principles of good and evil, which took a rigid form in later Zoroastrianism, may have been rejected by Zarathustra himself.[4]

The Zoroastrian system of ethics is of a very high order and is based on the teachings of the great prophet. The basis of ethics is religious: the Deity is the centre of moral goodness. 'Ahura Mazdā is the guarantor of the moral order of the universe, and the good is defined in terms of his will. He judges men, rewarding the good, punishing the evil.'[5] Man is free to choose his course of action. He has complete freedom of moral choice.

. . . The wise will choose that which is consonant with truth, light, and order, that which will identify him with the forces of good, and assist their triumph over the forces of evil. Man's part in the cosmic struggle, therefore, is to think good thoughts, speak good words, and perform good actions.[6]

In fact, Zoroastrian morality is summed up in the words 'good thoughts, good words, and good deeds'.[7] The moral life led by each person in this world has a direct relationship with the judgement that is to come after death. Zoroastrianism teaches that moral goodness will ultimately triumph over the moral evils in the world.

Within such a general framework we can better understand the fine Golden Rule statements in Zoroastrian scriptures.

The inclusive name for the sacred scriptures of Zoroastrianism is *Avesta*, perhaps meaning 'text' or 'basic text' or 'knowledge'. We often see the term *Zend-Avesta*; the term *Zend* ('explanation') means the translations, paraphrases and interpretations of the sacred texts in the Pahlavi language. Much of the original Avestan literature has been lost; of that which remains, the most important and earliest section is the *Yasna* ('service, sacrifice'). The *Yasna* contains the Gāthās (*Yasna* 28–34; 43–51; 53) meaning 'psalms' or 'songs', the oldest constituents of the *Avesta* and the only part attributable to Zarathustra himself. Therefore, if we seek information about the original form of the religion of Zarathustra, it is to the Gāthās that we must turn. When the present writer read the Gāthās he was struck by the sublimity, authority, and power of certain passages – yet knowing that the translation was not conveying the exalted sense of the original. A Golden Rule statement is claimed to be found therein:

> That which is good for all and any one,
> For whomsoever – that is good for me . . .
> What I hold good for self, I should for all.
> Only Law Universal is true Law. *[8]

The so-called Pahlavi books were mainly written in their present form in the ninth century AD and represent the views of the theologians of the last century of the Sassanian Empire.[9] These Pahlavi texts include, among others, the *Dādistañ-ī Dīnīk*, the *Sad Dar* and the *Dīnkard*. In the *Dādistān-ī Dīnīk*, a reference is perhaps made to an earlier Golden Rule statement or statements in Zoroastrianism:

And those of the primitive faith, the ancients of those acquainted with the religion, thus considered . . .
And this, too, was thus considered by them, that that nature only is good when it shall not do unto another whatever is not good for its own self . . .[10]

Despite the changes and chances of history and the alterations made by men of the original teachings of a religion, fundamental teachings of a religion often have an enduring quality.

In a section of the *Dīnkard* devoted chiefly to legal matters we are treated to yet another fine statement of the Rule. It is found in a section called the law of the Hamēmālistān ('accuser's code') which contains particulars about accusation as well as the limitation of the accusation of sin and the retribution for it. Here we read:

This, too, that when affliction has come upon a good *man*, the

---

* This passage illustrates many of the problems faced by the writer due to (a) unavailability of certain primary sources, (b) 'lifting' of statements from context in secondary sources, and (c) differences in translations of what are claimed to be statements of the Golden Rule. In fact, according to the reading of another translation of this same passage, it may not be regarded as containing the Rule at all:

Whoever brings untold bliss to others will be given that bliss by Ahura Mazda who ruleth at will. So in truth I crave from Thee Utayuiti, the Desire for Immortality, and Tevishi, the Desire for Perfection, so as to uphold Thy Divine Law. Bestow upon me, through Thy loving Aramaiti, that blessing of a perfect illumination – the life of the Good Mind.
And so, to such a man will be given the height of all blessedness of the blest. O most gloriously radiant Spirit, Mazda, grant me enlightenment, for Thou hast given to all, through Thy Law, the full measure of the Good Mind that each may enjoy unlimited bliss all the days of his long life. (Bode and Nanavutty (trans.), *Songs of Zarathustra: The Gathas*, p. 71.)

Scholars disagree widely about the interpretation of the Gāthās.

effort of every one, for removing that affliction, should continue just as though it happened to himself.

And when a good *man* is beaten through malice, the effort of every one, in demanding compensation for him from the smiter, should continue just as though it happened to himself.[11]

We will recall from the Hindu faith that in the *Manu-smṛti*, a collection of laws that, it is claimed, has a divine source, a Golden Rule statement also exists. This points again to the relationship between law in religion and the Golden Rule, a subject we will consider in more detail later on. Also, the view that '. . . the effort of every one, for removing that affliction, should continue *just as though it happened to himself*' (author's italics) and '. . . the effort of every one, in demanding compensation for him from the smiter, should continue *just as though it happened to himself*' (author's italics) is similar to the Taoist position in the *T'ai Shang Kan Ying P'ien* that one should 'pity the misfortunes of others; rejoice in the well-being of others; . . . *even as though you were in their place*' but different from the position found in some (but not all) statements from Hinduism, Jainism and Buddhism that you should conduct yourself according to the Golden Rule *because you think you are one with all other living things*.

And now we continue to explore one of the most fascinating yet fathomless realms in the boundless worlds of the Golden Rule. As we have seen before, the Rule not only involves interrelationships between man and man but also, if we take the broad view, between man and creation. Yet it could also involve relationships between (a) man and the messengers or prophets of God, (b) the messengers or prophets of God and God Himself, and (c) man and God – which can also include the messengers and the Holy Spirit as intermediaries. As we shall see in more detail in Chapters 15 and 16 on the Bahá'í Faith, this whole complex of relationships may be understood within the framework of the 'three worlds' concept of reality: the world of God, the world of Manifestation (prophethood) and the world of creation, all of which are linked together by the Holy Spirit.

In the *Sad Dar*, or *The Hundred Subjects*, we find Hôrmazd (Ohrmazd), who, as we noted earlier in this chapter, may be identified as the Holy Spirit or, after the passage of time in Zoroastrian history, with Ahura Mazdā Himself, in a mystical conversation with the prophet:

. . . The creator Hormazd says, 'O Zaratust! if thou wilt that thou become pure and saved, *and that* thou arrive at the place of the pure, do thou accomplish these two duties: –

One is this, that thou prefer the friendship of the spiritual *existence to that* of the worldly *one*, and consider the things of the world as contemptible and those of the spirit precious; on this account the glory of the world is sought with scorn, and do not thou let the spirit escape.

The second is this, that thou speak truly with every one and act justly with me, that is, whatever thou dost not approve for thyself do not approve for any one *else*; when thou hast acted in this manner thou art righteous.[12]

Authorities disagree as to whether the Golden Rule concerns only human beings in relation to one another or can also concern other beings that are intrinsically superior or inferior to human beings or are, in a sense, equal to human beings. One contributing factor towards this divergence is whether one happens to be a Christian or a Jain or a Hindu, etc. Another is whether a given thinker has Jesus Christ's statement of the Rule in Luke and Matthew uppermost in mind or whether his understanding of the possible scope of formulations of the Rule is different. But the writer's view is that, whether we view a statement approximating the Rule that involves relationships between unequals (such as God and man) as an example of the Rule or as a corollary to it, the fact remains that such statements throw much light on the possible scope of reciprocal relationships and our understanding and appreciation of the Rule itself. The philosopher Paul Weiss, in one of the rare scholarly articles devoted to the Golden Rule, explained:

. . . Because men have essential traits in common with any divinity that there may be, with animals, organic beings, and animate things, it is impossible to restrict (the usage of the term 'Golden Rule') to men without neglecting the fact that these others have values, and that there are situations in which they offer us a standard by which we can determine our actions on ourselves or on them.[13]

Very many followers of the world's revealed religions would agree that God offers us standards by which we can determine our actions towards Him and others. Our study of the Rule should, we think, throw light on our relationships with other human beings, other beings in creation, the prophets or messengers of God and the Almighty Himself.

11

In Judaism

Because the term 'the Golden Rule' has so often been associated with Christianity and Judaism, and since there are such very close links between the two religions, it is hardly surprising that, in the West, much more has been written about it in studies of Judaism and Christianity than in connection with other religions.

Judaism is an ancient religion, monotheistic in nature. But the word *Judaism* is not so ancient; it was first used about 100 BC in Graeco-Jewish literature to designate the religion of the Hebrews. The real beginning of the history of Israel is a matter of controversy. In one sense, it began with Jacob; in another, with Abraham, somewhere around 2000 BC, as the recipient of a divine call, revelation and promise; a prophet; the 'friend of God'.

Abraham is the *ideal* Israelite in the sense that he represents, especially in the view of the ethical prophets, what every Israelite should be, or should aspire to be – a man entirely obedient to God, a man of moral uprightness and devout faith.[1]

The second great figure in Judaism's long history was Moses (*c* 1500 BC), who had an enormous impact on mankind. In the Judaic tradition Moses is revered as its greatest prophet and teacher. Our prime interest here, however, is his activity, according to Hebrew tradition, not only as prophet but also as lawgiver.

The prophet who made known to the Hebrew tribes what had been revealed to him concerning the nature and purposes of the divine being, also made known to them in precise detail the pattern of life which this entailed for them as the beneficiaries of Yahweh's saving action. Here, in fact, we see another characteristic mark of Hebrew prophecy throughout its history, namely the insistence that to be the recipients of divine revelation means also for the Hebrews that their common life is to exhibit a certain pattern of ethical conduct.[2]

The 'Law of Moses' and the covenant that he made between the people of Israel and God were regarded by the authors of the historical books of the Jewish Bible, the prophets, and the author of the later book of Ezra as the cornerstone of Israel's existence.[3]

Absolutely fundamental in Judaism is belief in one God; there is no other God beside Him.

The very essence of Judaism is firmly stated in one sentence: 'Hear, O Israel: the Lord our God, the Lord is One!' It is the first prayer that a Jew learns as a child and it is the last prayer upon his lips before he dies.[4]

To followers of Judaism, man is an ethically responsible creature responsive to the presence of God. This responsiveness is particularly expressed in the relationship between people. The pattern of interpersonal relations is set down, within the limitations of the structures of the ancient Near East, in the pentateuchal legislation. No segment of society is free from ethical obligation.

A very significant affirmation in Judaism is that God is not only the source of ethical obligation but also is Himself the paradigm of it. This is expressed in Leviticus 19:1–2: 'And the Lord spake unto Moses, saying, Speak unto all the congregation of the children of Israel, and say unto them, Ye shall be holy: for I the Lord your God am holy.' Man should imitate divine holiness as the basis of human

behaviour in the ethical sphere. Judaism advocates three fundamental qualities for the good life: good deeds, enjoyment of living, and love of one's fellow man.[5]

Judaism's sacred scriptures are made up of twenty-four documents arranged in three groups: the Law, the Prophets and the Writings – documents that have inspired generations for centuries. This, the Hebrew Bible, is the cornerstone of Judaism. These documents are commonly known as the Old Testament in Christianity, where they have been rearranged into thirty-nine books. These scriptures represent a literary activity covering approximately one thousand years and had been practically completed before the lifetime of Jesus Christ, although the canon as it now exists did not come about until near the end of the first century AD.

The books of Genesis, Exodus, Leviticus, Numbers and Deuteronomy make up that portion of the Bible termed the Pentateuch, the five books of Moses. Judaism, for which the Pentateuch represents the most important of all revelations, calls it the Torah, the Law.*[6] Traditionally the authorship of the Torah is ascribed to Moses. But modern scholarship indicates that Moses kept some written records that served as the core of the growing corpus of law and tradition. The first five books of the Hebrew Bible can, therefore, be described as Mosaic in a general sense, but he cannot have written the whole of the Law.

Many people are familiar with the words 'an eye for an eye, a tooth for a tooth' (referred to in the chapter on traditional religions and societies). This phrase may be regarded as an expression of the principle of retaliation. Fewer are aware that it is found in no less than three instances in the

* '. . . The translation 'Law' for the Hebrew *Torah* gives a lop-sided and misleading impression. *Torah* really means guidance, instruction, teaching, etc. The word can mean the Pentateuch, the Bible, Revelation or traditional religion as a whole. It is only against the wider background of the Jewish theology of the "Word" as God's revealed Will that the translation "Law" acquires a measure of legitimacy.' (R. J. Zwi Werblowsky, 'Judaism, or the Religion of Israel', p. 17.)

Law: in Exodus, Leviticus and Deuteronomy. At this point the reader may ask: why include consideration of 'an eye for an eye, a tooth for a tooth' in a study of the Golden Rule? As we shall see in more detail shortly, scholars have noted that there are different levels of reciprocity that are traditionally expressed in four 'Rules': 'Iron', 'Tinsel', 'Silver' and 'Golden', with human reciprocity perhaps falling short of the 'Rule of Love'. (In fact, the range of the word *reciprocity* is vast.) In this traditional approach, then, the Iron Rule of 'an eye for an eye, a tooth for a tooth' is on the 'lowest level' of reciprocity.

However, when writers claim that the Iron Rule is on the lowest level of reciprocity, they sometimes neglect the fact that it was an improvement upon previous practice. In the *lex talionis* (law of retaliation) we have a basic law that has been handed down from extreme antiquity and still exists in modern form. Its wording must originally have meant that the offender should be punished in exactly the same manner as he had caused bodily harm to the other person.[7] The punishment, then, is not considered from the point of reparation (making good), but of retribution. Yet the law of equal retribution, which was widespread in the ancient world, put an end to the interminable continuance of blood-feuds as well as an end to the repayment of injuries with interest.[8] And even in the modern age, the principle of retribution is necessary for the maintenance of the moral order. Yet it is commonly regarded as impracticable and undesirable to enforce the Iron Rule of 'eye for eye, tooth for tooth' nowadays, conditions having changed since the days of the authorship of the Torah.

Although 'eye for eye, tooth for tooth' is found in Exodus 21:22–7 (in which an upper limit on punishment was stipulated) and Deuteronomy 19:16–21 (in which Hebrew law attempted to guard against perjured testimony by 'eye for eye' punishment), we shall cite here Leviticus

24:18–21 as containing a good example of the Iron Rule in the Law:

And he that killeth a beast shall make it good; beast for beast. And if a man cause a blemish in his neighbour; as he hath done, so shall it be done to him; breach for breach, eye for eye, tooth for tooth: as he hath caused a blemish in a man, so shall it be done to him *again*. And he that killeth a beast, he shall restore it: and he that killeth a man, he shall be put to death.

Different levels of reciprocity have been traditionally expressed in the four 'Rules'. Norman J. Bull terms them 'Rulers' rather than 'Rules':

The lowest level of reciprocity is the hard metal of iron retaliation – 'eye for eye, tooth for tooth' . . . This strict reciprocity was an advance on cruder moral customs, for its express purpose was to limit revenge. But it remains a primitive, low level of behaviour towards others . . .

An apparently higher level of reciprocity is expressed in the Tinsel Ruler – 'Treat others as they deserve'. Here, of course, concern with motives is introduced, so that this is a potential advance . . . It turns out, on closer inspection, to be little more than the Iron Ruler dressed up; no more, in fact, than tinsel – as a piece of tinsel, kept after Christmas, will visually symbolise . . .

A third level of reciprocity is summed up in the Silver Ruler – 'Do not do to others what you would not like them to do to you.' This is, of course, the negative form of the Golden Ruler, and in practice they might be explored together. [For example, all Golden Rule statements in Confucianism given previously, with the exception of Meng Tzŭ's, would be regarded as being on the Silver Rule level.] .

. . . This is certainly an advance on the two previous principles. But, being negative rather than positive, it makes no demands of active goodwill. It could be fulfilled by doing nothing at all. [Not all authorities would agree to this implied inferiority of the Silver Rule as compared to the Golden Rule. Some say it is superior, others claim there is no basic difference.

The present writer takes the latter position. We shall return to this problem later.]

   . . . The highest level of reciprocity is enshrined in the universal Golden Rule. Its particular form – '*What* ye would that men should do to you do ye even so to them' – is limited to specific actions. It is the general form that is of universal application – '*As* ye would that men should do to you do ye even so to them.'

Examples of this principle, whether in its negative Silver or positive Golden form, can be found in all races, religions and philosophies.[9]

We have seen that this last is doubtful, particularly if we include the many existing traditional religions in our investigations. But he makes the very significant point that the Golden Rule interpreted as the highest level of reciprocity has its limitations.

But is the Golden Rule enough? Calculations of human reciprocity can go so far. But there are two areas of profound moral concern where it would appear inadequate.

The first is the whole realm of human love. In the deepest relationships of love and friendship there is no place for calculation, for rules, for reciprocity. Love goes beyond them in giving without thought of return. It is deep-rooted in human nature. It is seen in the selfless love of a mother for her child; in the care of a 'good father' for his children, a concept that is far more than merely biological; in the love of friends for each other that dissolves self-interest in mutual identity; and in human sympathy for neighbours, seen at its best in time of trouble.

But who exactly is my neighbour? The famous parable [of the 'Good Samaritan' in the New Testament of the Christian Bible] gives the answer. Does the Golden Rule apply to everyone – to enemies, to aliens, to foreigners? In theory, perhaps, the answer is 'Yes'. But in practice it tends to be limited to 'us', and to be ignored in our dealings with 'them'. In this second area, too, something more than reciprocity is involved. Only love is adequate for it. All love must have its roots in feeling for others, in human sympathy. But this kind of love is more than feeling. It is an attitude of goodwill that at its highest is concerned for, and so cares for, enemies – those, that is, for whom there are no good feelings.

This second kind of love makes the highest demands upon human nature, for it has no feelings as such to motivate and to support it . . . We find it in the universal compassion taught by the Buddha . . . We find it in the love ethic of Jesus, in His demand for positive and unlimited caring, so that my neighbour is everyone. Here, too, is a close link with religion. For ultimately universal love can only be motivated by a conviction that all human beings are one family. Natural reason can of itself reach out to an ideal concept of the brotherhood of man. Natural weakness requires a motive strong enough to put it into practice by overcoming all the prejudices that divide mankind into 'us' and 'them'.[10]

Others would maintain that one can reciprocate love for love and, at an even higher level, lack of love with love. This exalted love for not only friends but enemies – whether or not it is at a level of reciprocity – is basically at one with the principle of universal unrequiting goodness. We shall return to these issues later.

But the Pentateuch contains more than instances of the Iron Rule. In Leviticus 19:18 is what some writers regard as a Golden Rule statement in which love, the highest expression of the Golden Rule, is given great prominence. Leviticus 19:18 has been set forth in Rabbinic teaching, in addition to the command to model behaviour on the ways of God, as one of two outstanding guides or principles for the moral life.[11] 'Thou shalt love thy neighbour as thyself: I am the Lord.'* Rabbis have disagreed whether this statement includes the greatest principle of the Torah.

'Thou shalt love thy neighbour as thyself' (Lev. 19:18). Rabbi

---

* References to this passage are found in the New Testament of the Christian Bible in Matthew 22:37–40, Luke 10:25–37, Romans 13:8–10, Galatians 5:13–15 and James 2:1–13.

Akiba says: This is the great principle of the Torah. Ben Azzai says: 'This is the book of the generations of Adam:

> In the day that God created man, in the likeness of God made He him' (Gen. 5:1) –
> this is a principle greater than that.[12]

Interestingly, the term *neighbour* is a fluid one whose meaning has changed with time. It has been maintained, with an impressive array of evidence, that at the time of Jesus Christ the non-Israelite was not comprehended in the command to love one's neighbour.[13] But there are Jewish scholars who disagree with this and maintain that the command was taken to apply to all men. Placing this particular controversy aside, we can say that today, in our rapidly shrinking world, *neighbour* is gradually becoming understood in a much more universal sense. For those who believe in universal love and the brotherhood of man, all human beings are truly our neighbours!

A further connection between Leviticus 19:18 and the Golden Rule is found in the *Palestinian Targum*, in which the negative form is inserted at the end of Leviticus 19:18, making the latter part of that verse read: 'But you shall love your neighbour; what is hateful to yourself you shall not do to him; I am Jehovah.'[14]

As the centuries passed, a large body of commentary developed around the sacred law. In the year AD 70 the Romans destroyed Jerusalem and the Temple, and subsequently the Jews were dispersed to many lands. This mass of commentaries and commentaries on the accepted commentaries continued to grow after the dispersion. Much of this was written down to form two collections, the Mishna and the Gemarra, and finally these were joined to form what is known at present as the Jewish *Talmud* ('study' or 'learning').[15] The *Talmud* appeared in two different forms, the *Palestinian Talmud* (or *Jerusalem Talmud*), which is the earliest of the two collections, and the *Babylonian Talmud* (otherwise known as *The Talmud*), which was concluded in the sixth century AD. The importance of the *Talmud* in Rabbinic Judaism was explained by a modern Jewish scholar:

Theologically speaking, the Talmud as the 'Oral Law' is second only to the Bible. But as a matter of fact it may almost be said to be primary since Rabbinic Judaism can view the Bible only *through* the Talmud whose categories of thought, theological perspective and legal interpretations are normative and determine the understanding of Scripture. [16]

However, in the modern age there are a variety of views about the authority of the *Talmud* particularly between the followers of liberal Judaism and orthodox Judaism.

In a portion of the *Babylonian Talmud* known as Shabbath there is a much-cited Golden Rule statement associated with the venerated teacher Hillel the Elder (*c.* 60 BC to AD 10), founder of the 'House (or School) of Hillel'. His colleague, Shammai, headed another school which held differing views from that of Hillel's. Hillel came to Jerusalem in about 40 BC and roughly between 30 BC and AD 10 taught in that city. [17] The reader may realise at this point that Hillel was living in Jerusalem during the boyhood of Jesus Christ; the possible relationship of their Golden Rule statements will be discussed in the next chapter. One scholar maintains that the Golden Rule approximation given by Hillel was a version of Leviticus 19:18. [18]

A certain heathen came to Shammai and said to him:
Convert me provided that you teach me the entire Torah
    while I stand on one foot.
Shammai drove him away with the builder's cubit which
    was in his hand.
He went to Hillel who said to him:
What is hateful to you, do not do to your neighbour:
    that is the entire Torah;

the rest is commentary;
go and learn it.*[19]

This delightful incident as recorded in the *Talmud* has reinforced the view that the Golden Rule is a leading contender as the outstanding guide to conduct in Jewish thought.

The importance of Golden Rule statements in or associated with Judaism is further illustrated by their existence in the Mishna (*Aboth* II, 10 and 12); the Old Testament Apocrypha (*Tobit* 4:14–15 and *Ecclesiasticus* 31:15); the Pseudepigraphia (*Testament of Naphtali* (Hebrew text) 1:6); the Targum (*Jer. Targum* on Leviticus 19:18); Philo Judaeus' *Hypothetica* 7:6; the *Wisdom of Ahikar* (Armenian text) 2:88; Maimonodes' *Sefer ha-Mitzvoth* (H. Heller edition, Petrokoff, 1914, p. 64) and *Mishneh Torah, Hilkot Ebel XIV*, .. One interesting example is from the *Letter of Aristeas*. This is an account, in Greek, of the miraculous translation of Hebrew scriptures into Greek, known as the *Septuagint*, dated between 200 BC and AD 33.[20] Here the negative and the positive versions of the Golden Rule are combined in some advice to a king:

As thou desirest that evils not befall thee, but to partake of all that is good, thou shouldst act in this spirit to thy subjects and to offenders, and shouldst very gently admonish such as are virtuous; for God draws all men (to Him) by gentleness.[21]

---

* 'By commentary Hillel meant the body of literature that resulted from a definition of love to one's fellow-man, the significance of enjoyment of living, and what constitutes good deeds.' (S. A. Nigosian, *World Religions*, p. 35.)

12

In Christianity

Christianity stands among the world's great religions while its founder, Jesus Christ, has had a profound and lasting influence on untold millions of people in many parts of the world. The exact date of his birth, however, is a matter of dispute among scholars. Our knowledge of his life is derived from the four Gospels and a few other references in the New Testament of the Christian Bible. He was born in a Jewish society in what is now Israel and taught in that part of the world; after his tragic death, his faith spread throughout much of the earth, particularly in the West.

The concept of the 'essence of Christianity' has been expressed in various statements ever since its first conceptual definition by the fifth-century Gallic monk Vincent of Lérins: the Christian faith is 'what has been believed everywhere, always, and by all'.

Christians maintain that for an understanding of the principles of Christianity and the maintenance of a Christian life, the Bible stands as the primary source. The Protestants assert that it comprises the 39 books of the Old Testament and the 27 books of the New Testament, but the Bible of the Greek and Latin Churches also contains fourteen other books appended to the Old Testament and known as the Apocrypha by Protestants and Deutercanonical by Roman Catholics. The New Testament records the life and teachings of Jesus Christ and the thoughts and experiences of some of his early disciples, and is shared by all the Christian churches and sects. The books of the New Testament came into being after the lifetime of Jesus Christ.

What is presumably the earliest of Paul's letters, the first letter to the Thessalonians, was written circa 50 AD, St. Mark's gospel circa 70 AD and the other gospels somewhat later. All the writings of the New Testament had been completed by about 120 AD [Other authorities give 150 AD] . . .

It is certain that the canon [of the New Testament] had been fixed by the end of the second century (the Muratorian Canon).[1]

As is the case with other religions, thinkers who have attempted to expound upon Christian ethics and morality in a systematic manner have not always agreed with each other. This process has developed historically.

It was not till the 4th century AD that the first attempt was made to offer anything like a systematic exposition of Christian morality; and nine centuries more had passed away before a genuinely philosophic intellect [St Thomas Aquinas], trained by a full study of the greatest Greek thinker, undertook to give complete scientific form to the ethical doctrine of the Catholic Church.[2]

The following brief presentation of Christian ethics and morality as presently understood by Christians therefore possesses a number of limitations.

Christian ethics have strong connections with the Jewish inheritance, including a reverential acceptance of the Ten Commandments. Christian ethics are set forth in Jesus' teaching and illustrated by his example.

At the very core of Christian teaching is belief in the existence of God. Christian morality essentially presupposes God's existence.[3]

Christian ethics differs fundamentally from all forms of secular ethics . . . in this respect, that its morality is made to spring directly out of the relation in which an individual stands to God.[4]

God is infinite Goodness Itself. God is Love. Love is the key to Christian morality and the essential motivating principle of Christian good conduct. From a Christian point of view, the backbone of all moral attitudes is the love of God through Christ.

A fundamental guideline for good conduct in Christianity is found in the words of Jesus Christ given in the New Testament book of Matthew. When one of the Pharisees who was a lawyer asked, 'Teacher, what is the great commandment in the law?' Jesus replied (Matthew 22:37–40):

Thou shalt love the Lord thy God with all thy heart, and with all thy soul, and with all thy mind. This is the first and great commandment. And the second *is* like unto it, Thou shalt love thy neighbour as thyself. On these two commandments hang all the law and the prophets.

Jesus was evidently referring here firstly to Deuteronomy 6:5: 'And thou shalt love the Lord thy God with all thine heart, and with all thy soul, and with all thy might.' Also, we recall the beautiful Golden Rule statement given in Leviticus 19:18 that is regarded as being such a fundamental moral guide in Judaism: 'Thou shalt love thy neighbour as thyself: I am the Lord.' But here Jesus teaches the fundamental oneness of the two: 'And the second is like unto it . . .' We have also noted how the concept of the scope of the word *neighbour* has changed with the passage of time from application to a narrow range of associates to, in this modern age, the whole of mankind. (A similar transformation has been occurring with the word *brother*.) Such a change must have been gradually taking place in the minds of Christians ever since the life and times of Jesus Christ, and may very well have accelerated during the past 100–200 years. Jesus himself taught the wide application of this Golden Rule principle in the famous story of the 'Good Samaritan' (Luke 10:25–37):

And, behold, a certain lawyer stood up, and tempted him, saying, Master, what shall I do to inherit eternal life? He said unto him, What is written in the law? how readest thou? And he answering said, Thou shalt love the Lord thy God with all thy heart, and with all thy soul, and with all thy strength, and with all thy mind; and thy neighbour as thyself. And he said unto him, Thou hast answered right: this do, and thou shalt live. But he, willing to justify himself, said unto Jesus, And who is my neighbour? And Jesus answering said, A certain *man* went down from Jerusalem to Jericho, and fell among thieves, which stripped him of his raiment, and wounded *him*, and departed, leaving *him* half dead. And by chance there came down a certain priest that way: and when he saw him, he passed by on the other side. And likewise a Levite, when he was at the place, came and looked *on him*, and passed by on the other side. But a certain Samaritan, as he journeyed, came where he was: and when he saw him, he had compassion *on him*, and went to *him*, and bound up his wounds, pouring in oil and wine, and set him on his own beast, and brought him to an inn, and took care of him. And on the morrow when he departed, he took out two pence, and gave *them* to the host, and said unto him, Take care of him; and whatsoever thou spendest more, when I come again, I will repay thee. Which now of these three, thinkest thou, was neighbour unto him that fell among the thieves? And he said, He that shewed mercy on him. Then said Jesus unto him, Go, and do thou likewise.

The Samaritan was a non-Jew whereas the priest and Levite were believers. But the fundamental importance of love is not confined to Judaism and Christianity among the world's religions, as we shall see later.

Christian thinkers have observed the close links between love and many other virtues such as charity, humility, selflessness, and forgiveness. Such virtues were not included in the moral standard of the Graeco-Roman world during the lifetime of Jesus. Christian ethics and morality are fundamental in the preparation of the soul for the afterlife. Also, both Jews and Christians believe that, in spite of disbelief and disobedience on the part of men, God's moral rule will at some time in the future be fully established throughout the whole world.[5]

Although our treatment of the subject must again be brief, we can confidently say that Christian ethical teaching, including the teaching of the Golden Rule, has taken a prominent place in Christian religious education since the earliest days and has continued to the present. For example, in early Christian times a person who aspired to become a believer was, after an examination, admitted to the catechumenate and 'made a Christian'. The catechumen was, as the name implies, one distinctively under instruction. The subject-matter of the catechesis was both moral and doctrinal. In the earlier stage of the catechumenate the moral teaching predominated; after this instruction had been completed, other teaching followed.

An example of the type of elementary moral education given might be found in a Jewish work entitled the *Two Ways*, which was adopted by the Christian *Didache Apostolorum* (Teaching Doctrine of the Twelve Apostles)* for the purpose of a prebaptismal catechesis (4 *Didache* 1–5; *Epistle of Barnabas* 18–20).

Its teaching falls into two parts, the 'Way of Life' and the 'Way of Death'. The 'Way of Life' is described in a series of precepts, with considerable repetition, designed apparently to impress the principles on the mind of the catechumen by presenting them from different points of view and in different applications. The first section begins with the precept to love God, and to love one's

---

* The *Didache* was an early Christian writing that was excluded from the New Testament canon.

neighbour as oneself, and expands and illustrates the latter from the negative 'Golden Rule' and the Sermon on the Mount.[6]

A modern example of the stress given to the Golden Rule in Christian education is found in the Church Catechism and the Order of Confirmation in the Book of Common Prayer of the Church of England.

The principle was frequently quoted by prominent Christians through the years: Clement, Pope Fabian, Cyprian, Tertullian, Chrysostom, St Augustine, etc.* Modern writers on Christianity often refer to it. In short, the Golden Rule has made an indelible mark on the momentous history of the Christian faith.

As is well known, the message of Jesus Christ was directed firstly to Jews; later, through the efforts of St Paul and others, Christianity spread widely among non-Jews. Although throughout the centuries some Jews have become Christians, very many have not. This is, in the view of the present writer, at the core of the controversy that has raged for many years whether Jesus Christ's ethical teachings, including the Golden Rule, differed significantly from contemporary Jewish ethical teachings. The Golden Rule in Christianity is commonly thought of as being expressed in Matthew 7:12 ('Therefore all things whatsoever ye would that men should do to you, do ye even so to them: for this is the law and the prophets') and Luke 6:31 ('And as ye would that men should do to you, do ye also to them likewise'), but it is less commonly known that it is also found in a negative form in the New Testament in the Bezan text of Acts 15:20, 29 as well as, according to some authorities, in Romans 13:10. The Bezan text of Acts 15:20, 29 adds the following words to the prohibitions enforced upon the gentile Christians: 20: 'And whatsoever they do not wish to be done to them, not to do that to others'; 29: 'And

---

* For further details see McArthur, 'Golden Rule', p. 137.

whatsoever you do not wish to be done to yourselves, do not to another.'[7] The claim has been made that the negative form of the Golden Rule lies behind Romans 13:10. St Paul first cites Leviticus 19:18: 'Thou shalt love thy neighbour as thyself', and then adds his explanation of it: 'Love worketh no ill to his neighbour', in a form reminiscent of the *Targum*.[8]

Both the version in Matthew and the version in Luke appear within important contexts: in Matthew it is the Sermon on the Mount, and in Luke the Sermon on the Plain. In fact, many Christian scholars state that the essence of Christian morality and ethics is contained in the Sermon on the Mount. Both the Sermon on the Mount and the Sermon on the Plain may be presumed to have belonged to the 'Q' document, the earlier tradition of Jesus' sayings that the two Gospels have in common.[9]

Thus the versions of Matthew and Luke are apparently related to each other. Luke reports that Jesus spoke of love as the principle of conduct and pointed out how it may operate in concrete situations (Luke 6:27–30). He then presents the Golden Rule as the summation of conduct.[10] But Matthew's reported words of Jesus after the Rule – 'for this is the law and the prophets' – are not included by Luke.

In the present writer's view, it is a great pity that some scholars seem to have been more preoccupied with the alleged 'superiority' or 'inferiority' of this or that religion and/or, more specifically, this or that Golden Rule statement than with such issues as the beneficial effects these religions and the various Golden Rule versions have had upon the peoples of the world. He fears that in some cases the motivation has been to attack another faith while defending one's own. But other scholars have been, perhaps in their own minds, more equitable in their judgement.

Firstly, let us examine the charges that there is no origi-

nality in the teachings of Jesus, that those teachings that
were conceivably his seem to be of a piece with Jewish
teaching, that Jesus Christ did not come to preach any
brand-new morality and that the ethics of Jesus agree strik-
ingly if compared in detail with contemporary Jewish
ethical teaching. An example will suffice:

The attempt on the part of Christian scholars to discover in the
teaching of Jesus some new teaching about ethics or morals has
completely, or almost completely, broken down. Those modern
Jewish scholars who have busied themselves with a comparison
between the ethical teaching of Jesus and the ethical teaching of
the rabbis have given this judgement, that there is no single moral
aphorism recorded as spoken by Jesus which cannot be paralleled,
and often verbally paralleled, in rabbinic literature. With this
conclusion Christian scholars working in the field of rabbinics are
showing more and more agreement . . . Even the Golden Rule
has its parallel in rabbinic teaching.[11]

On the other hand, some authors assert that there is
something new in the Christian ethic, and they refer to the
Golden Rule. In this connection, they often maintain that
Jesus' version of the Rule was positive, whereas other
versions were negative.

It is very important to note that the Christian ethic is a positive
ethic. This is to say that the Christian ethic on the whole tells us
rather what to do than what not to do.

   The Ten Commandments [in the Old Testament] are on the
whole *Thou shalt not's*. In one particular commandment – not one
of the Ten Commandments – this is of the first importance. This
is in what is usually known as the Golden Rule. In its negative
form the Golden Rule is to be met with in many systems of ethics:
Don't do to others what you would not like them to do to you.
But the Christian version of it is positive: Do to others what you
would like them to do to you (Matthew 7.12). The Christian
version is much the more demanding. It is not so very difficult to
abstain from doing things. But the Christian demand is not

simply that we abstain from doing things to others, but that we actively do to them what we would wish them to do to us.

This is the Christian doctrine of love. We have to note very carefully the word the Christian ethic uses for love. It is the word agapē . . . It means an undefeatable attitude of goodwill . . .[12]

The argument can continue swinging back and forth when we note the retort that despite the positive form in Matthew and Luke, a negative version was circulating in the Christian tradition – particularly as found in the Bezan text of Acts 15:20, 29 and in Romans 13:10. We can also dismiss any claims that positive versions of the Rule did not exist before the time of Jesus Christ. The most relevant example here is that in Leviticus 19:18: 'Thou shalt love thy neighbour as thyself.'

In fact, the alleged 'superiority' or 'inferiority' of the positive and negative versions of the Golden Rule, a dispute that has involved other religions besides Judaism and Christianity, has vexed religionists, philosophers, and others for many years. The reader will recognise that this dispute is closely connected with the Silver Rule / Golden Rule issue investigated in the last chapter. Christians and Jews have probably been more embroiled in this controversy than anyone else.

One pivot upon which this and even wider issues swing is whether Jesus Christ was a divine revelator. This has obviously influenced the thinking of scholars who have either accepted or rejected the view that his 'positive' statement(s) were superior to other 'negative' versions. We recall that Hillel was a very prominent Jewish teacher who lived in Jerusalem during the boyhood of Jesus, and we also recall that his version of the Rule was negative:

> What is hateful to you, do not do to your neighbour:
> that is the entire Torah;
> the rest is commentary;
> go and learn it.

Now, some thinkers no doubt have deduced from their investigations of this and other statements that Jesus Christ had been influenced by various moral and ethical teachings from Judaism, including one or more Golden Rule versions (including Hillel's) and was merely repeating them with a few minor changes here and there – such as the changeover from the negative version (such as Hillel's) to a positive one. The further inference here is that these moral and ethical teachings were not, therefore, divinely inspired but were given by a (perhaps) admittedly great man.

Interestingly enough, virtually the same charges have been brought against Muḥammad by Christian thinkers. In addition, the great Bahá'í scholar Mírzá Abu'l-Faḍl referred to one of several charges against the Bahá'í Faith that had been made by a Christian writer: 'That the Bahá'í Religion is not able to show anything better or superior to other religions; in a word, what new things has Bahá'u'lláh brought which are not found in the Christian religion; and what is the need of distinction?' a question that was followed by ten pages of detailed points explaining what is new in the Bahá'í Faith that is not in Christianity[13] – details that can be added to considerably by others. In short, what we see here in the case of Jesus Christ is fundamentally the same as that endured by the founders of a number of the world's religions: they have not only suffered at the hands of their detractors during their lifetimes but after their deaths accusations have been made against them, attributing objectionable qualities to them; their teachings have been criticised and, in some cases, misinterpreted; the claim has been made that their religions have brought nothing new or, conversely, that the new teachings are immoral, unethical, contrary to the religious law, etc. – charges usually brought by certain intellectuals, scholars, religious leaders and others among the older religions. (On the other hand, those who cause a founder to suffer most may be the adherents of his own faith.) So the defenders of Jesus Christ's ethics and his version of the Golden Rule have been engaged in a struggle that, historically, has repeated itself. Tragically, such disputes have all too often been part of a chain of events in which millions have died and suffered in the name of religion.

Therefore, we see that charges of 'borrowing' of teachings by the founder of a religion, or that he was 'influenced by' teachings given in an older faith are particularly serious and can have many repercussions. Did Jesus Christ merely 'borrow' the Golden Rule from Hillel and put it in positive form? or intelligently combine this particular 'borrowing' with a number of others from Judaism and, perhaps, other sources to come up with his version of the Rule? On the other hand, what if it is asserted that Jesus Christ was a divinely-inspired revelator and that his teachings were from the Almighty? Such a position is taken by a very large segment of humanity – among others, Christians, Muslims, Bahá'ís, and, undoubtedly, a good number of Hindus. Now a whole new light shines on the controversy. Christians and others can cite, among other things, the words of Jesus Christ given in the New Testament to support this. For example, in John 12:44–5, 49–50 he is reported to have said:

He who believes in me, believes not in me but in him who sent me. And he who sees me sees him who sent me . . . For I have not spoken on my own authority; the Father who sent me has himself given me commandment what to say and what to speak. And I know that his commandment is eternal life. What I say, therefore, I say as the Father has bidden me.

Further, many of the founders of the great religions have avowed that their revelation and teachings are from God. For instance, such assertions have been made by Muḥammad[14] and Bahá'u'lláh.[15]

Is the Almighty, in the process of revelation of His truths through His chosen mouthpieces, in any need of 'borrowing' or 'being influenced by' *anybody*? Yet He may, in His infinite wisdom, reveal similar teachings such as the Golden Rule through several revelators or prophets or messengers, teachings that may, as time passes and conditions change, increase in sophistication and encourage and reflect man's gradual spiritual, moral, ethical and social development. We shall return to this important theme in a moment.

The reader has already discovered that the dispute over whether the positive version of the Golden Rule as given by Jesus Christ is superior to negative formulations is far from simply resolved. Some have firmly placed themselves on one side of the fence, while others have been content to remain on the opposite side. But a good number of writers, evidently both Jews and Christians, have seemed uncertain about the alleged superiority or inferiority of Jesus' positive version of the Rule.

Debate has centred around the respective merits of the two [positive and negative] versions; some scholars contending that the positive is superior since it makes greater demands on the altruism of the obedient hearer, while others have praised the negative version on the grounds that it 'goes deeper into the heart of the problem' (Abrahams). Chrysostom, *Concerning the Statutes*, XIII 7, quotes both versions, commenting that one requires 'a departure from iniquity', the other 'the exercise of virtue'.[16]

St. Paul seems to have regarded the two forms as interchangeable.[17]

Again, in a careful study of the merits and demerits of the negative versus the positive versions of the Rule, confined virtually to the Jewish–Christian context, George Brockwell King claimed that if the origin of the negative rule goes back to the commandment of Leviticus 19:18, that of the positive rule may well lie there also. 'This is all the more probable as we see Jesus placing the seal of his commendation on the command of Leviticus 19:18 in Luke 10: 27, 28.'[18] King goes on:

One wonders if a great deal too much has not been made of the superiority of the positive over the negative golden rule, especially in the light of their possible relation the one to the other and to Lev. 19:18, as revealed in the foregoing study . . . Jesus on occasion gave his teaching in negative form . . . As Friedlander remarks,* most laws are given in the negative form. The negative golden rule teaches a negative morality only in the mind of him who wishes to persuade himself that it does . . .

It is time, then, that the dispute as to the superiority of positive over negative golden rule came to an end. There is no basis for extravagant praise of the positive any more than there is ground for Abraham's assertion that the negative is the more funda-mental of the two, 'going deeper into the heart of the problem'. Basically they are the same, in idea as in origin.[19]

In a more general article, the philosopher Marcus G. Singer, after a study of the issue, concluded that the negative and positive formulations of the Rule are logically and morally equivalent but not psychologically or rhetorically equiva-lent, the difference being one of emphasis.[20]

Again, the question of whether the positive form states a higher moral ideal than the negative has been dismissed as being of little moment.[21] A Jewish writer made the comment: 'To my mind the issue is that of value, not of priority . . .'[22] The present writer would whole-heartedly agree that nit-picking about superiority or inferiority, originality or borrowing, etc. can divert people from more fundamental and vital issues such as the role of the Golden Rule in changing the thoughts, words and deeds of people for the better in societies throughout the globe. In this

* G. Friedlander, *The Jewish Sources of the Sermon on the Mount*, p. 235.

connection, the highly respected Bahá'í scholar George Townshend made a significant point when he wrote:

All [Jesus Christ's] commandments, negative and positive, were such as to put an end to estrangement and to promote affection, harmony, and concord. He sought in every way to cleanse men's hearts of selfishness and to educate them from self-centredness to world-centredness.[23]

Yet another school of thought that has gained increasing importance since the pioneering work of the German philosopher and theologian Friedrich Schleiermacher around the beginning of the nineteenth century holds that it is impossible to make a sharp cleavage between Christianity and the pre-Christian spiritual world and stresses not only the unity of Christianity with Judaism but the fundamental unity of religion in general. The great Anglo-German scholar of religion, Max Müller, asserted, 'There is only one eternal and universal religion standing above, beneath, and beyond all religions to which they all belong or can belong.'[24] From this point of view, similarities of Golden Rule versions found in so many of the world's religions, including Judaism and Christianity, are an indication of that fundamental unity, and issues such as negative versus positive versions, superiority or inferiority, Golden versus Silver are of lesser significance.

In fact, among Christian theologians of all periods, there have been some who have noted the revelation of God in the non-Christian world. For instance, the Swedish Lutheran Archbishop Nathan Söderblom (1866–1931) declared on his deathbed, 'God lives, I can prove it by the history of religions.'[25] The same attitude towards other faiths is true for pious men and women of thought in, we would assume, all the great religions of the world.

But if there is essential unity of religion, if there is in reality one religion, is that religion static, unchanging? Or does it develop, evolve, progress? If we wish to take this issue, firstly, from a Christian point of view, we could very well say *Yes* – religion evolves up to a point. Examples may be given from the sayings of Jesus Christ demonstrating how his teachings, in certain instances, appear to be an advancement over traditional principles in Judaism. For instance, he said (Matthew 5:38–9):

Ye have heard that it hath been said, an eye for an eye and a tooth for a tooth: but I say unto you, that ye resist not evil: but whosoever shall smite thee on thy right cheek, turn to him the other also.

The view can be set forth here that Jesus Christ was calling upon men to live up to a new standard. The contention has also been made that the greatness of Jesus Christ lies in his giving to his formulation of the Golden Rule a universal application rather than a narrow national one as given by his contemporaries. From this point of view, since religion progressed up to the coming of Jesus Christ, the Golden Rule as given by him in Matthew and Luke would build upon and add to the older formulations. Conditions had changed. Although the positive form of the Rule had existed previous to Jesus Christ, the time in history had arrived for it to be given by him in this form in accordance with the needs of those millions who were to benefit from his teachings. Also, did not mankind *need* the Golden Rule again, this time in a positive form, due to the moral and ethical degradation in society at that time? Various authorities have acknowledged 'the decline that had set in in the religious, the spiritual, the cultural, and the moral life of the Jewish people, at the time of the appearance of Jesus Christ'.[26] Was the Golden Rule not then provided for man by a loving, infinitely wise God, through the instrumentality of Jesus Christ? This, then, can be a position that many Christians would accept.

But this is definitely not the end of the matter. To most Christians, the end of all revelation came to man through Jesus Christ. Nothing is needed at present or in future except Christianity and the Christian Bible. One of several Christian rationales for the finality of the revelation of Jesus Christ was provided to the author by a Christian scholar:

The whole issue of Christ's revelation being final and complete must be seen in the context of the Christian interpretation of the doctrine of the Holy Trinity. Jesus Christ is believed to be the Son of the Father, there being nothing that the Father does and knows and loves that the Son does not do and know and love, except bringing forth the Son. Jesus must therefore have expressed somehow the whole Father; then what more is there to reveal? At the same time Paul says that no one can call God Father except in the Spirit of Christ. To the Christian, therefore, if Muḥammad and Bahá'u'lláh speak in unity with Christ, and do not scatter but gather with him, then even Christians can learn from them and be edified. Admittedly, this is not stressed much in the Christian tradition, but it would seem to be in the spirit of Christ himself. It does not, however, fit into the doctrine of progressive revelation on the theological level; it only fits a theory of progressive understanding.[27]

The finality of the revelation of Jesus Christ is not accepted by Muslims. One among several reasons for this position is that the doctrine of the Trinity is obviously not accepted in the Qur'án. The unity of God is stressed in Islám. In Súrih 5:76–7 of the Qur'án we read:

> They do blaspheme who say:
> God is one of three
> In a Trinity: for there is
> No god except One God.
> If they desist not
> From their word (of blasphemy),
> Verily a grievous penalty
> Will befall the blasphemers

Among them.
Why turn they not to God
And seek His forgiveness?
For God is Oft-forgiving,
Most Merciful.[28]

The Christian interpretation that Jesus Christ's revelation is final is also not accepted in the Bahá'í Holy Writings. In the Bahá'í Faith the oneness and unity of God is again given much emphasis, but it is a very subtle, deep subject that we cannot go into in detail.* An authoritative Bahá'í view of the doctrine of the Trinity was given by 'Abdu'l-Bahá.[29] We can give only a portion of it here:

The Divine Reality which is purified and sanctified from the understanding of human beings and which can never be imagined by the people of wisdom and of intelligence, is exempt from all conception. That Lordly Reality admits of no division; for division and multiplicity are properties of creatures which are contingent existences, and not accidents which happen to the self-existent.

The Divine Reality is sanctified from singleness, then how much more from plurality. The descent of that Lordly Reality into conditions and degrees would be equivalent to imperfection and contrary to perfection, and is therefore absolutely impossible. It perpetually has been, and is, in the exaltation of holiness and sanctity.[30]

The Sonship station of Jesus Christ is accepted in the Bahá'í Faith[31] but it is not linked to any rationale for the finality of his revelation. (Again, this is a subject we cannot treat in detail.)

Thus, the Christian view of the finality of the revelation of Jesus Christ based upon the doctrine of the Trinity is not accepted in either Islám or the Bahá'í Faith. We must stress that neither Islám nor the Bahá'í Faith are in disagreement

---

* See, for example, Bahá'u'lláh, *Gleanings from the Writings of Bahá'u'lláh*, pp. 165–6, 186–93, 260–61; 335–7.

here with what would be regarded as fundamental truths and teachings given by Jesus Christ himself, but with interpretations given to his teachings developed by certain of his followers.

Further, does the Christian view of the finality of the revelation of Jesus Christ mean that, among other things, the moral and ethical teachings of Jesus, including the Golden Rule, need not be given again and built upon and further developed by later revelators to meet the needs of an evolving humanity – that what mankind has in the Christian Bible is all man needs for as long as he exists, no matter how much the world changes? The whole matter is complicated further by one of the most controversial issues within Christianity, the return of Christ. In over 250 places in the New Testament (the books of which were completed by about AD 120–50) the certainty and consequences of Christ's return are indicated. But what about the instances where he said *another* would come? For example, he declared (John 16:7):

Nevertheless I tell you the truth; It is expedient for you that I go away: for if I go not away, the Comforter will not come unto you . . .

and (John 16:12–13):

I have yet many things to say unto you, but ye cannot bear them now. Howbeit when he, the Spirit of truth, is come, he will guide you into all truth.

To explain these prophecies by saying they do not refer to a person is a weak theological argument and cannot be substantiated. Details of this highly complex issue are outside the scope of our subject.* But the possibility of

* For a Bahá'í view see William Sears, *Thief in the Night* (London: George Ronald, 1961), and George Townshend, *The Promise of All Ages* (London: George Ronald, 1961).

further revelations after the first coming of Jesus Christ is an issue that Christians cannot ignore.

Belief in one religion that is progressive is found clearly in Islám and the Bahá'í Faith, and this is virtually inseparable from what is termed in both religions *progressive revelation*. (Again, it is not our intention here to go into this matter in detail.) In the Qur'án, Súrih 42:13, we read:

> The same religion has He
> Established for you as that
> Which He enjoined on Noah –
> The which We have sent
> By inspiration to thee –
> And that which We enjoined
> On Abraham, Moses, and Jesus:
> Namely, that ye should remain
> Steadfast in Religion, and make
> No divisions therein . . .[32]

And in Súrih 2:106 we find:

> None of Our revelations
> Do We abrogate
> Or cause to be forgotten,
> But We substitute
> Something better or similar:
> Knowest thou not that God
> Hath power over all things?[33]

Muslims, then, can very well take the view that God's revelations, including, among many other things, various statements of the Golden Rule, *Christian and otherwise*, have always been basically the same, but their form may differ according to the needs and exigencies of the time. Again, Golden Rule controversies between Jews and Christians about superiority or inferiority, etc. fade into the background. The interpretations and controversies of men shrink into insignificance compared to the expression of the

Will of God. In God's wisdom He brings formulations of the Golden Rule and other teachings within a revelation 'better or similar' than those given in previous revelations. The question arises, of course, as to who is a revelator and who is not.

But, with Muslims, progressive revelation is taken just so far. Muslims, like Christians, typically claim finality for their religion. We shall return to this problem in the next chapter.

The essential unity of religion and progressive revelation as understood from a Bahá'í view has profound implications for our understanding of the boundless worlds of the Golden Rule and of the various approaches that can be taken towards the controversies about the superiority of Jesus Christ's ethics over older ethical systems as well as the superiority of his Golden Rule statements over others. But to present a concise yet comprehensive Bahá'í view of this broad yet subtle subject within an appropriate context is a formidable task indeed. Fortunately, a most helpful introduction can be found in the following three statements by the Guardian of the Bahá'í Faith, Shoghi Effendi:

The fundamental principle enunciated by Bahá'u'lláh, the followers of His Faith firmly believe, is that religious truth is not absolute but relative, that Divine Revelation is a continuous and progressive process, that all the great religions of the world are divine in origin, that their basic principles are in complete harmony, that their aims and purposes are one and the same, that their teachings are but facets of one truth, that their functions are complementary, that they differ only in the non-essential aspects of their doctrines, and that their missions represent successive stages in the spiritual evolution of human society.[34]

The Faith standing identified with the name of Bahá'u'lláh disclaims any intention to belittle any of the Prophets gone before Him, to whittle down any of their teachings, to obscure, however slightly, the radiance of their Revelations, to oust them from the hearts of their followers, to abrogate the fundamentals of their doctrines, to discard any of their revealed Books, or to suppress the legitimate aspirations of their adherents. Repudiating the claim of any religion to be the final revelation of God to man, disclaiming finality for His own Revelation, Bahá'u'lláh inculcates the basic principle of the relativity of religious truth, the continuity of Divine Revelation, the progressiveness of religious experience. His aim is to widen the basis of all revealed religions and to unravel the mysteries of their scriptures. He insists on the unqualified recognition of the unity of their purpose, restates the eternal verities they enshrine, coordinates their functions, distinguishes the essential and the authentic from the nonessential and spurious in their teachings, separates the God-given truths from the priest-prompted superstitions, and on this as a basis proclaims the possibility, and even prophesies the inevitability, of their unification, and the consummation of their highest hopes.[35]

Just as the organic evolution of mankind has been slow and gradual, and involved successively the unification of the family, the tribe, the city-state, and the nation, so has the light vouchsafed by the Revelation of God, at various states in the evolution of religion, and reflected in the successive Dispensations of the past, been slow and progressive. Indeed the measure of Divine Revelation, in every age, has been adapted to, and commensurate with, the degree of social progress achieved in that age by a constantly evolving humanity.

'It hath been decreed by Us', explains Bahá'u'lláh, 'that the Word of God, and all the potentialities thereof, shall be manifested unto men in strict conformity with such conditions as have been foreordained by Him Who is the All-Knowing, the All-Wise.'[36]

Bahá'í belief is that God has sent Manifestations since time immemorial. The names of many who appeared in remote antiquity have been lost. But in the past 5,000 years or so, the Manifestations who have appeared have included Krishna, Abraham, Moses, Zarathustra, Buddha, Jesus Christ, Muḥammad, the Báb (the forerunner of Bahá'u'lláh) and Bahá'u'lláh. Bahá'ís are to have the deepest love and respect for them all. Other lesser figures have appeared who have aided man's spiritual, moral, and ethical development, a contribution that should be deeply appreciated. For instance, Confucius is regarded as being the founder of a moral system and a great reformer.[37] The Manifestations were possessed of the Holy Spirit and acted as intermediaries between God and man; it follows that all the great religions are in essence one.

The foregoing is, although incomplete, an accepted Bahá'í view of the essential unity of religion and progressive revelation. The following is largely the present writer's own views, according to the limitations of his understanding, of how these principles may be applied to the controversies he is discussing.

Perhaps the most crucial issue raised is that Jesus Christ brought no new ethical teachings and did not come to preach any new morality, a charge that many have endeavoured to refute. Now, if all revealed religions are essentially one, if both Judaism and Christianity are, in essence, revealed religions, and if all revealed religions bring moral and ethical teachings, teachings that are of divine origin (as distinct from the man-made ones that have crept into many religions), a case can begin to be built up in favour of the view that the fundamental basis of ethics and morals in religion is the same. From this point of view, then, the ethics and morals taught and exemplified by Jesus Christ were in essence neither 'superior' nor 'inferior' to those taught by Abraham, Moses, and other prophets in the Judaic tradition. In fact, the basic principles as given to man by these mighty figures, including, we would assume, their fundamental and essential moral and ethical teachings, *would naturally be harmonious.* Both Jews and Christians might do well to investigate and come to appreciate the fundamental unity and harmony as well as the beauties and beneficial impact of the essential moral and ethical teachings in both faiths – but they should also do the same for all the great faiths, as they are essentially one.

Yet it is obvious that mankind gradually evolved during the years between the appearance of Abraham, Moses and Jesus Christ. This gradual change would be reflected in gradual changes in moral and ethical teachings and in laws. One would expect, then, some change to be apparent between the moral and ethical teachings of Jesus Christ and those found in the Hebrew Bible, particularly those that could with some confidence be attributed directly to Moses. The moral and ethical teachings of both were linked with their common aim, were facets of the same fundamental truth and were complementary to (not competitive with) each other. The measure of 'Divine Revelation' brought by both Moses and Jesus Christ had been 'adapted to, and commensurate with, the degree of social progress achieved in that age by a constantly evolving humanity'. This, from one point of view, would again make the moral and ethical teachings of Jesus Christ, including the Golden Rule, neither 'superior' nor 'inferior' to those divinely inspired moral and ethical teachings to be found in Judaism at that time, but they would *of necessity* have to reflect the gradual changes that had occurred in society.

If a newer revealed religion's moral and ethical teachings happen, in some instances, to appear to be on a somewhat higher level than those in the older, it is not in detriment to the older. If they happen to be more or less identical, it is not in detriment to the newer. Both are highly valuable, respected and *needed*.

That many of Jesus Christ's moral and ethical teachings were not radically different from those found in Judaism at that time, in fact were often more or less identical, can also be explained by the need for revitalisation, reinforcement and restatement of teachings that were badly needed in a society that had decayed morally and socially. People needed to be reminded and effectively taught over and over again what was right and what was wrong. This had to be based on the background and previous knowledge of the people to whom it was directed. They may not have been able to grasp something that was radically different.

In this connection, in the Bahá'í view of progressive revelation, a religion founded by a Manifestation of God is revealed, grows, reaches a peak (which is typically accompanied by the emergence of a great civilisation), begins to decay, and continues gradually to lose its power. The unity and fellowship it inspires are dispersed, there is a tendency for sects to proliferate, materialism supplants spirituality, and hatred and intolerance replace love. God, in His wisdom, sends another Manifestation with another religion (which is an integral part of the one basic religion from God) with, among other things, moral and ethical teachings that may in some cases be virtually identical to, in other instances somewhat different from, those brought by the previous Manifestation, according to the needs of society at that time. From a Bahá'í view, this is basically what happened before and at the time of the appearance of Jesus Christ.

The controversies over Jesus' ethical and moral teachings and his version of the Golden Rule fade into further insignificance in view of the Bahá'í teaching that progressive revelation is, in essence, a process without beginning and without end. There is *no* finality in the process. Future Manifestations will continue to appear after Bahá'u'lláh, the first one after the expiration of a full thousand years. Mankind is to be led towards and achieve ever higher levels of morality in the future. We would, therefore, assume that the Golden Rule itself could be understood and practised on ever higher levels. Would not mankind generally understand and practise ever-progressing dimensions of love? Also, if man comes into contact with intelligent, moral and ethical beings and other presently unknown creatures from other parts of the universe in the future, how might this affect man's understanding and practice of the Golden Rule? Phrases such as 'do unto others' or 'universal love' would be understood in a radically different way from the way they are today. Might this not involve a reformulation of the Golden Rule by a future Manifestation or Manifestations? In brief, Jews and Christians involved in the controversies about Jesus' ethical and moral teachings and his Golden Rule may be so intent on two proximate trees that they are failing to see the mighty forest.

13

In Islám

The word *Islám* is Arabic and connotes submission, surrender, obedience. From a Muslim point of view, it is incorrect to term the religion 'Muḥammadanism'; a Muslim is 'one who submits' to the will of God. The followers of the great world religion of Islám are widespread, with most living at present in parts of Asia and Africa.

From a Muslim view, the origins of Islám may be traced back to the creation of man, as 'submission' has always characterised man's relationship to God. In the sixth century AD in Arabia the Prophet Muḥammad appeared. Muḥammad was born in Mecca either in AD 570 or 571 and received his divine call in 609 or 610. The proclamation of the revelation to his countrymen was positively received by a growing number but also brought abuse, ridicule, and persecution, particularly from leaders of religion. These circumstances led to the migration of Muḥammad and some of his followers on 24 September 622 from Mecca to Medina, a migration known in Arabic as the *Hijra*. This is the year from which all Muslim calendars are dated. Muslims believe that God revealed the holy book the Qur'án through Muḥammad over a period of 23 years until shortly before his passing in AD 632.

The essence of the faith taught by Muḥammad is given in Súrih 2 ('The Cow'), verse 172, of the Qur'án, revealed partly at Mecca and largely at Medina:

It is not piety, that you turn your faces
 to the East and to the West.
  True piety is this:
to believe in God, and the Last Day,
the angels, the Book, and the Prophets,
to give of one's substance, however cherished,
 to kinsmen, and orphans,
the needy, the traveller, beggars,
 and to ransom the slave,
to perform the prayer [*ṣalát*], to pay the alms [*zakát*].
And they who fulfil their covenant
when they have engaged in a covenant,
 and endure with fortitude
 misfortune, hardship, and peril,
these are they who are true in their faith,
these are the truly godfearing.[1]

'Three fundamental principles – recognition of the unity, the oneness, the transcendence of God; recognition of the Messengership of Muḥammad (which by its very nature entails belief, as well, in all the Messengers of the past); belief in the Day of Resurrection – are accepted by all Muslims, of whatever persuasion, as pillars of their faith.'[2] Islám imposes just five obligations on the faithful: they must affirm that there is no god but God and that Muḥammad is the Apostle of God; they must pray five times a day; they must fast one month (of Ramaḍan) out of the year; they must pay the obligatory alms annually; and they must, if they are able, make one pilgrimage to Mecca in their lifetime.

Islám is a strictly monotheistic religion: belief in one God is its foundation. It teaches not only the existence of God but the existence of His names and attributes such as the Creator, the Merciful, the Lord of Bounties, the Most Kind, the Forgiving, and the Beneficent. The qualities and attributes that a man must possess, if he wishes to pursue the way of Islám, can be cultivated and developed only out of deep knowledge of the attributes of God; the knowledge of God's attributes purifies a person's mind and soul, his beliefs, morals and actions.[3]

Islám teaches a way of living. Both the Qur'án and the Ḥadíth (Traditions) contain numerous admirable teachings enjoining a very high standard of conduct.

Moral values are mentioned in almost all the passages of the Qur'án . . . Some of these repeatedly mentioned are: sincerity, honesty, humility, chastity, meekness, charity, politeness, love, forgiveness, goodness, courage, sympathy, justice, straightforwardness, obedience, appreciation, kindness, and steadfastness.

The dimensions of morality cover a number of aspects. These are mainly the relationship between man and God, man and man, man and other creatures, and man and his internal self. The moral values in Islam teach man to desist from inflicting injury upon his fellowmen, and also encourage him to do good to others.[4]

The essential unity of religion and progressive revelation as linked to the development of morality in humanity is taught in Islám. A Muslim writer has declared that all the prophets who made their appearance from time to time propagated Islám and asked people to live a life of obedience and submission to God; this is what constitutes al-Din (Faith).[5] He continues:

Apart from this Din there is the Shari'ah or the detailed code of conduct or the canons comprising ways and modes of worship, standards of morals and life, laws that allow and prescribe, that judge between right and wrong. Such canon law has been undergoing amendments from time to time and though each Prophet had the same Din, he brought with him a different Shari'ah that would suit the conditions of his own people and time. This served the purpose of training different people over all ages for a better civilisation and equipping them with better morals. The process ended with the advent of Muhammad, the last Prophet (peace be upon him) who brought with him the final code which was to apply to all mankind for all times to come. *Din* has undergone no change, but now all the previous *Shari'ahs* stand abrogated in view of the comprehensive *Shari'ah* that Muhammad (peace be upon him) has brought with him. This is the climax or the final of the great process of training that was started at the dawn of the human era.[6]

Again, from a Bahá'í view, the question may be asked: Does this mean that the moral and ethical teachings of Muhammad, including the Golden Rule, need never be given again and/or built upon and further developed by later revelators to meet the needs of an evolving humanity, and that what we have in the Qur'án is all man needs for as long as he exists, no matter how much the world changes? Has not the world changed enormously just in the past 150 years? Does not mankind's present moral degeneration require a global moral regeneration? And how long will man continue to exist in this material universe in the future? 1,000,000 years? 3,000,000 years? Will the *Bhagavad-Gítá* or the Bible or the Qur'án contain *everything* that man requires for religion then?

The controversy centres on the typical Muslim interpretation of the term 'Seal of the Prophets' as applied to Muhammad. To Muslims, this basically means that He was the last of the prophets and no other shall appear after Him. To them, the divine source of guidance remains the Qur'án, and, as it is the last revelation, it is logically a book for all time. But in the Bahá'í Faith the claim is made that Muhammad's revelation, although very great, is not a final revelation from God and that Muhammad is the 'Seal of the Prophets' in a different sense from that in which Muslims commonly understand it that Muhammad never said that he was the last messenger (*Rasul*) from God.* And both Muslims and Bahá'ís assert to Christians that Jesus Christ

---

* Bahá'u'lláh elucidates the term 'Seal of the Prophets' at considerable length in the *Kitáb-i-Íqán*.

was not the last great revelator from God. All these issues
have enormous implications for the future evolution of
ethics and morality and the Golden Rule for the human
race, as we shall touch upon again later. But to delve into all
these complex questions in great depth is beyond the scope
of this book.

Yet there is no question about the fact that the Qur'án is
the primary foundation of the religion of Islám and that
through the ages it has been the object of great veneration.
Arabic is a most subtle and beautiful language, and the
Qur'án contains such an exquisite expression of it that all
translations into English have failed to convey its subtlety
and beauty. Yet even in translation the reader, Muslim or
non-Muslim, can be profoundly moved by its contents.

Scholars agree that the Qur'án contains the accurate
teachings of Muḥammad from God. It is divided into 114
chapters (súrihs) containing discourses on a very wide range
of subjects.

In his *The Meaning of the Glorious Qur'án*, Abdullah Yusuf
Ali has translated the entire Qur'án, including the following
from Súrih 83, verses 1–6, 'The Unjust' or 'Those Who
Give Short Measure or Weight', revealed at Mecca:

> Woe to those
> That deal in fraud, –
> Those who, when they
> Have to receive by measure
> From men, exact full measure,
> But when they have
> To give by measure
> Or weight to men,
> Give less than due.
> Do they not think
> That they will be called
> To account? –
> On a Mighty Day,

A Day when (all) mankind
Will stand before
The Lord of the Worlds?[7]

In his commentary, Yusuf Ali gives his view as to the connection between this passage and the Golden Rule, a connection that may already be apparent to the reader:

'Fraud' must here be taken in a widely general sense. It covers giving short measure or short weight, but it covers much more than that. The next two verses make it clear that it is the spirit of injustice that is condemned, – giving too little and asking too much. This may be shown in commercial dealings, where a man exacts a higher standard in his own favour than he is willing to concede as against him. In domestic or social matters an individual or group may ask for honour, or respect, or services which he or they are not willing to give on their side in similar circumstances. It is worse than one-sided selfishness: for it is double injustice. But it is worst of all in religion or spiritual life: with what face can a man ask for Mercy or Love from God when he is unwilling to give it to his fellow-men? In one aspect this is a statement of the Golden Rule, 'Do as you would be done by'. But it is more fully expressed. You must give in full what is due from you, whether you expect or wish to receive full consideration from the other side or not.[8]

In Súrih 59, 'Exile' or 'The Emigration', revealed at Medina, we find yet another example in the annals of religion of the principle of universal unrequiting goodness. The principle requires, as the reader will recall, that a person prefer others before himself. The rewards and benefits of this practice are referred to in this Súrih, verse 9:

But those who
Before them, had homes
(In Medina)
And had adopted the Faith, –
Show their affection to such
As came to them for refuge,

And entertain no desire
In their hearts for things
Given to the (latter),
But given them preference
Over themselves, even though
Poverty was their (own lot).
And those saved from
The covetousness of their own
Souls, – they are the ones
That achieve prosperity.[9]

This passage will be discussed again in Chapter 16 on the Bahá'í Faith, as Bahá'u'lláh has referred to it.

In addition to the Qur'án, the Hadíth are a fertile source of Golden Rule statements in Islám; they record Traditions of what Muḥammad did and said. The two main branches in Islám, the Shí'ah and the Sunní, do not share exactly the same Hadíth: Shí'ahs include the recorded Traditions of the holy Imáms. The Hadíth are held in great reverence, next to the Qur'án, throughout the whole Muslim world; Muslim law as well as Muslim practice are to a great extent founded on them.

The question of the credibility of each Tradition has been of great importance to Muslims throughout the years, for the Traditions were not all considered of equal value by Muslim scholars but were divided into categories according to certain criteria. Numerous collections of Traditions were made, and some of these works have gained almost canonical standing among later Muslims.[10] Six works came to be generally recognised among orthodox Muslims as authoritative. They all arose during the third century AH.* Two of these, the collections by al-Bukhārī (died AH 256 / AD 870) and Muslim (died AH 261 / AD 875) were held in particularly high esteem. In both collections the following statement is included:

---

* anno Hegirae: the year of the Hijra, AD 622.

None of you [truly] believes until he wishes for his brother what he wishes for himself.[11]

Other Golden Rule statements attributed to Muḥammad are found in the *Sukhanán-i-Muḥammad*:

1. Seek for mankind that of which you are desirous for yourself, that you may be a believer; Treat well as a neighbour the one who lives near you, that you may be a Muslim.
2. That which you want for yourself seek for mankind.
3. The most righteous of men is the one who is glad that men should have what is pleasing to himself, and who dislikes for them what is for him disagreeable.
4. Whatever you abhor for yourself, abhor it also for others, and whatever you desire for yourself desire also for others.[12]

Unfortunately, the same basic controversies rage between some Muslims and Christians over the alleged comparative superiority or inferiority of the ethical and moral teachings of Jesus Christ and Muḥammad as those between Jesus Christ and such teachings in the Hebrew Bible. Much of what we have already said in general about these issues in the last chapter would apply here as well. But in this case, the charge has been made that certain Muslims 'borrowed' statements from Christian sources and incorporated them into the *Ḥadíth*. Also, it has been contended that there was a widespread and long-continued Christian influence on Muslim ethical thought. (Exactly the same thing has been said about the Jewish influence on Christian ethical thought. Granted that these influences have existed, the question arises: if there is only one religion, who is influencing whom?) A Christian writer not always sympathetic to Islám states:

During the first three centuries of Islam the sayings ascribed to Muhammad were still in a fluid state and there were renegade

Christians and others who wished to strengthen the Muslim polemic in Christian communities. They made their influence felt in the formulation of sayings which they ascribed to Muhammad that would not be ethically unlike those of Christ.[13]

He then gives the above four citations from the *Sukhanán-i-Muḥammad* as examples of the point. The present writer's view is that the question of the origins of Traditions ascribed to Muḥammad is such a complex and difficult one that passing any kind of certain judgement on many of them, particularly after the expiration of so many years, would be very risky. However, in view of the very high status given to al-Bukhārī's and Muslim's collections, which are the original sources of the fine Golden Rule statement given previously, he doubts very much that that particular statement could possibly have originated from a 'renegade Christian'!

As in Confucianism, Zoroastrianism, Judaism, Christianity, and other religions, Golden Rule statements made in the earliest days of Islám had a long-range impact throughout the history of the religion. Ibn Maskawaihi (d. AD 1030) prepared an outline of the science of ethics. This book, *Tahdhib al-Akhláq wa Taṭhír al-A'ráq* ('The Correction of Dispositions and the Cleansing of Veins') is the most important book on philosophical ethics in Muslim literature.[14] In Chapter V, on the 'Kinds of Love', it is stated that in their associations with one another men should be bound by ties of love and united in true friendship so that each will wish for his friend what he wants for himself.[15]

Another example of the pervading influence of Golden Rule statements in Islám is found among the writings of the Ṣúfís. As this movement developed historically its emphasis came to centre on the attainment of inner illumination and, especially, union with God. Generally, mystics in the great religions such as Buddhism, Christianity and

Islám have certain characteristics in common. Among the writings of the Ṣúfís we find:

> Whate'er thou likest not *for thine own self*,
> For any person else, too, like it not.[16]

In past chapters we have noted over and over again how reciprocity is related to the Golden Rule – for example, in Confucianism, where the relationship is given considerable prominence. The Prophet Muḥammad is reported in one *Hadíth* to have said, 'There should be neither harming nor reciprocating harm.'[17] This and other statements in the Qur'án and *Hadíth* would tend to reinforce the view held by many thinkers that Islám is a religion that, in essence, aims at the establishment and strengthening of peaceful human relationships.

Today, humanity's greatest failure is in the field of human relations. We recall the passage from the Qur'án, Súrih 83:1–6 quoted on pp. 100–101:

> Do they not think
> That they will be called to account? –
> On a Mighty Day,
> A Day when (all) mankind
> Will stand before
> The Lord of the Worlds?

Here then in Islám we find the highly significant notion of judgement: that those who fail to practise the Golden Rule in its various ramifications will be called to account before Almighty God.

One Western authority has written about what he calls the condition or principle of 'reversibility', a principle that has obvious connections with the Golden Rule.

Doing evil is doing to another person what it would be contrary to reason for him to do to himself. Harming another, hurting another, doing to another what he dislikes having done to him are the specific forms this takes. Killing, cruelty, inflicting pain, maiming, torturing, deceiving, cheating, rape, adultery are instances of this sort of behavior. They all violate the condition of 'reversibility', that is, that the behavior in question must be acceptable to a person whether he is at the 'giving' or 'receiving' end of it.

. . . All nonreversible behavior is morally wrong . . .

The principle of reversibility does not merely impose certain prohibitions on a moral agent, but also certain positive injunctions. It is, for instance, wrong . . . not to help another person when he is in need and when we are in a position to help him . . . [18]

Not all thinkers would agree with the principle of 'reversibility' or with the details given above.[19] But failure to practise the Golden Rule in one form or another is obviously a fundamental moral issue.

A psychiatrist, Bernard L. Diamond, writing about what he terms the sociopathic* personality – a personality frequently seen by students of crime and delinquency – maintains that all individuals suffering from sociopathic personality disorders are characterised by the defective quality of their interpersonal relationships.[20] Their capacity to love is much impaired. As a result, they lack the compassionate, ethical and moral values intrinsic to a mature relationship. Such individuals commit asocial or anti-social acts that lead them into conflict with society. The sociopath may lack the capacity for identification with others, or identifies in only limited or circumscribed ways, or his identification is shifting or transient. In the absence of identification, the biblical injunction 'love thy neighbour as thyself' and the Golden Rule – 'Therefore all things whatsoever ye would that men should do to you do ye even so to them' – become completely meaningless and incomprehensible.[21] Some individuals' lack of capacity to identify

---

* The term *sociopath* is a fluid one. The terms *psychopath* and *antisocial personality* are often used synonymously with *sociopath*, but their meanings can also differ.

with others has been a lifelong, consistent pattern, while for others the condition is temporary.

Diamond also explains, from his point of view, some of the circumstances which can temporarily transform compassionate people into unfeeling sociopaths, willing, even eager, to abandon the Golden Rule.

(1) Propaganda which labels and portrays the victim in derogatory words and images, implying that he is subhuman, bestial, dangerous, and perverted; using racist names . . . (2) Unfamiliar places where one must cope with persons who are different and strange, whose language one does not understand; soldiers fighting in foreign countries are especially vulnerable to this effect. (3) Fear, despair, grave uncertainty, and demoralization; seemingly, the effects are similar whether the cause is social and political oppression, economic deprivation, or participation in combat. (4) Exhilarated excitement associated with uninhibited group action . . . (5) The willingness (or sometimes the necessity) to be blindly obedient to authority. The atrocities of war and of political oppression are experienced as being permissible when commanded by higher authority. (6) Physical factors – pain, fatigue, extreme hunger, drug or alcohol intoxication, the physical need to survive. (7) Appeals to higher, supernatural motives; violence and dehumanization in the name of religion, patriotism, nationalism, and ideology can supersede human compassion. The Golden Rule is suspended because the destruction of the victim is experienced as a sacrifice to the loftier goal. Paradoxically, as we achieve a greater identification with our fellow crusaders and other true believers, we lose all compassion for the heretic who does not share our convictions. As Erik Erikson has so well said: 'In the name of high moral principles all the vindictiveness of derision, of torture, and of mass extinction can be employed.'[22]

Neither temporary nor consistent 'sociopaths' who violate the Golden Rule *in the name of religion or otherwise* should be produced by any religious persuasion. This problem is particularly highlighted by the fact that the Golden Rule is such a fundamental teaching among the world's religions. Bahá'u'lláh warned:

The Great Being saith: O ye children of men! The fundamental purpose animating the Faith of God and His Religion is to safeguard the interests and promote the unity of the human race, and to foster the spirit of love and fellowship amongst men. Suffer it not to become a source of dissension and discord, of hate and enmity. This is the straight Path, the fixed and immovable foundation.[23]

Religion should increase the capacity of mankind to love; to live in a harmonious society; to be more unified so that differences and strangeness are reduced; to uphold the principle of justice; to be free of prejudices, of religious, patriotic, nationalistic and ideological intolerance, of fanaticism and of bigotry; to abstain from selfishness, murder, cruelty and deception; to be free of war and oppression. Then mankind would be made up of people who would practise the Golden Rule on a very different level from that of today. A thorough transformation of society through the power of religion is the cure for these diseases.

Up to this point we have been discussing the problem of failure to practise the Golden Rule largely on the level of interpersonal relationships, with a statement from the Qur'án as our starting point. But the Golden Rule must also be understood in the context of broad social relations. Religion in the modern age can also address itself to the problem on a global scale. As if the complexity of this problem on the person-to-person level were not enough, its ramifications on the international and global scale present us with issues of bewildering intricacy. Yet some generalisations may be made. One interesting attempt along these lines was made by the Nobel Prize-winning scientist Linus Pauling:

It is characteristic of the world of today, as of all earlier times, that the principles of morality that apply to the actions of individual beings do not apply to the actions of nations. There is a tremendous difference between personal morality and national morality. Whereas most men and women, all over the world, accept the principles of ethics and morality that have been formulated and expounded by the great philosophers and religious leaders of the past, and behave in accordance with them [*sic*], nations act in ways that are determined almost entirely by considerations of selfish national interest. . .

The immorality of nations is associated with the retention of the principle of national sovereignty, which is the rejection of world law, the refusal to formulate and accept a set of dispute-settling rules based upon the principles of ethics and morality. Nations have instead depended upon war or the threat of war as the mechanism for the settling of disputes . . .

But what is the Golden Rule for *nations* in their mutual intercourse? It seems to be: 'Do unto others as evilly as you can find an excuse for' . . .

I believe that the time has now come for the nations of the world to co-operate in the solution of world problems, and to work together for the welfare of the whole of humanity.[24]

It is precisely the awareness of such immoral and unethical relationships between nations, achieving their possible climax in another all-out world war utilising weapons that can destroy a large part of the human race, that has been a major factor in the thinking of men of vision who seek the establishment of an effective world government, a government dedicated to world peace, world unity and a new world order. But the initial establishment of such a government would not be an automatic panacea for all humanity's ills. Such a government would have to be served, we think, by individuals educated to the highest moral and ethical standards, including the Golden Rule in both its interpersonal and broad social aspects. This whole issue may lend support to the view that there is need for a global regeneration of religion so that this 'new man' may be produced in the future.

Moral and ethical perfection for the whole of humanity and perfect understanding and practice of the Golden Rule in the future by all people seem unrealistic and unattainable goals. K'ung-fu-tse himself admitted he could not live up to the Rule. There may always be some evil men in the world. But man has to strive towards achieving 'an ever-advancing civilisation'. People of all faiths could unite towards this aim.

14

In Sikhism

Sikhs regard Sikhism as a religion. Sikhism grew out of an environment in India some hundreds of years ago in which Hindus and Muslims lived side by side but followed practices in their respective religions that were not mutually acceptable – such as caste, idol-worship, pilgrimage, reverence for sacred buildings, legalism and ritualism. Today the vast majority of Sikhs live in India.

The origins of Sikhism go much further back than the time of the great reformer Guru Nának (AD 1469–1538). The ideas of one of the great religious poets of India (and of the world), the weaver Kabír (AD 1440–1518) may have made an impression on Nának. Kabír is regarded as a pupil of the famous saint Rámánanda, who was influenced by the eleventh-century philosopher Rámánuja. Kabír's main aim, apparently, was to convince both Muslims and Hindus that they were children of the same Father and were thus brothers in their common humanity.[1] His hymns convey a message of trust in God and brotherly love.

Whether Kabír directly influenced Nának is a matter of dispute. But they both brought the same basic message: there is no Hindu and no Muslim in the sight of God. Thus, Sikhism was a conscious attempt to harmonise the two most powerful religions in India. However, while the Sikhs combine elements from both Hinduism and Islám (particularly Ṣúfístic Islám), they have become a separate community with their own sacred book, form of worship and succession of Gurus (religious leaders). The first of these was Guru Nának, who organised a body of followers who were called *Sikhs*, or 'disciples'. The fifth was Guru Arjan Dev (AD 1563–1606). The tenth and last was Guru Govind Singh, who, after years of persecution of the believers and the execution of two Gurus, transformed the originally peaceful Sikhs into a quasi-military group.

Sikhs accept the Hindu theory of *saṃsára* – birth, death and rebirth – and *karma*, whereby the nature of a person's life is determined by his actions in a previous life. Human birth is the individual's one opportunity to escape *saṃsára* and attain salvation. The guidance of the guru towards the attainment of *mokṣa* – release – is essential.

But combined with Hindu elements is the straight-forward monotheism of Islám. The unity of God is empha-sised in Sikhism. This is stressed in the opening lines of Nának's celebrated morning prayer, which are known as the *Mul Mantra* ('root belief') of Sikhism. Sikh scriptures contain many names, both Hindu and Muslim, for God, and Sikhism emphasises the constant repetition of the name of God and the divine hymns of the Gurus. This cleanses the soul of sin and conquers the source of evil, the ego. When tamed, the ego becomes a means to overcome lust, anger, greed, attachment and pride. The ultimate aim of the process is the attainment of a state of absolute bliss.

The foundations of Sikh ethics are explained further:

Sikh ethics are based upon three fundamental concepts – first, that the principles kirt karo, nam japo and vand cako, work, worship, and charity, should dominate one's complete life. Second, that self-reliance (haumai) is the great enemy of God-realisation and that it manifests itself in lust, anger, greed, materialism and pride. Activities which result from any of these vices should be avoided. This is best done by practising the virtues of contentment, patience, the service of others and humility which is considered to be the lynch pin of them all. Guru Nanak once remarked, 'Sweetness and humility are the essence of all virtues' (*Adi Granth* 470). Finally, it is as a householder (grihastha), a member of a family, not as one who has withdrawn from the world either to become a student or a hermit, that a Sikh should explore the meaning of God-realisation.[2]

The sacred book of the Sikhs is the *Granth*. The title *Granth* is a common noun derived ultimately from Sanskrit, meaning 'book', but as a technical term it is used to designate pre-eminently 'the Book'.[3] Its full name is the *Adi Granth Sahib*. The original *Granth* was largely compiled in 1603–4 by Guru Arjan Dev from material that had come from Nának and the intervening teachers. A few short pieces by the ninth and tenth Gurus were added later. The contents of the *Granth* reflect the unifying aim of Sikhism, being taken from thirty-seven authors including seven of the ten Gurus, various Sikh bards, and other highly respected Muslim and Hindu figures, the latter including Kabír and Rámánanda.

The Sikhs regard the *Granth* as possessing absolute authority. Although idol worship is not practised in their faith, Sikhs pay divine honours to the Book. Within the Sikhs' central shrine, the so-called Golden Temple (Darbar Sahib) of Amritsar, India, an extremely beautiful building, the *Granth* is preserved with great reverence.

In the *Granth*, 'Gauri Bawan Akhari', from Guru Arjan Dev, we find what has been interpreted as a Golden Rule statement:

> Be thou not estranged from another,
> For, in every heart, Pervades the Lord.[4]

and in the 'Siḍh-gosht', composed by Guru Nának, we read:

Says Nānak, he exalts himself, for sure,
Who sees him–Self, One Self, in all that lives. *[5]

Kabír is the source of this Golden Rule version:

As thou deemest thyself so deem others. [6]

So Sikhism as well has its honoured place in the boundless worlds of the Golden Rule.

---

* Another translation reads:
  When one dieth to the self, one becometh a know all; and
    knoweth within the All-merciful God.
  He alone attaineth Glory who See-eth himself in all Life.
        (Dr Gopal Singh (trans.), *Sri Guru-Granth Sahib*, Vol. III, p. 897)

15

In the Bahá'í Faith
An Introduction

The dream of a universal religion is an ancient one, a common characteristic among the teachings of the world's religions. Is this widespread desire and expectation never to come to fulfilment? Or are the trials and sufferings and the ferments in thought experienced by mankind in our age intrinsic to a divine plan for the eventual attainment of that aim?

The present writer has searched for a satisfactory explanation by scholars for the enormous changes in the world that have taken place since about the beginning of the 19th century. For instance, nearly all the trained scientists who ever lived since the origin of man are alive today. We are also experiencing at present the modern 'knowledge explosion', in which mankind's accumulated knowledge is increasing exponentially. Perhaps the world historian Arnold Toynbee came closest to the mark when he attributed this change to the *Zeitgeist*, the 'spirit of the times'.

There *is* a new spirit in the world. People are dissatisfied with the old order – with some older religious beliefs, with every national education system in the world, with present trends in global economic development, with the constant threat of nuclear annihilation, etc. We have seen how moral relationships are becoming universalised. A new, universal religion that will lift mankind from the mire of our present-day way of life is becoming the ardent of desire of souls in both East and West, North and South.

The demand of our day is for a religion within which virtuous actions, heroic character, the practice of the Golden Rule, are seen to be their own reward, and the security of the future is in well-doing and well-being in the present.

Such a religion develops human brotherhood that is more inclusive than sectarian.[1]

The attainment of this universal religion is regarded as inseparable from the achievement of the unity of mankind and a new society. The prominent Indian philosopher Sarvepalli Radhakrishnan wrote:

We cannot afford to waver in our determination that the whole of Humanity shall remain a united people, where Moslem and Christian, Buddhist and Hindu shall stand together, bound by a common devotion not to something behind but to something ahead, not to a racial past or a geographical unit, but to a great dream of a world society with a universal religion of which the historical faiths are but branches.[2]

If there were one universal faith adhered to with devotion by the human race, and if the Golden Rule were prominent in its teachings, the Rule would become universal in a new sense throughout the globe.

Bahá'ís make the extraordinary claim that the divine faiths of the past have laid the groundwork and that their own faith has appeared as the realisation of that religion – thus fulfilling the desires and dreams of poets and philosophers and pious men of vision throughout the centuries and the expectations of the prophets of the past. But this view is not based on the opinions of ordinary men. It is based on the teachings of Bahá'u'lláh and his forerunner, the Báb.

The Bahá'í Faith is a revealed religion, claims to be the world religion of the future and enjoys official recognition and legal status in an increasing and already considerable number of countries as a new and independent religion. The Faith is not a sect of any other religion such as Islám and is not a philosophy.

The word *Bahá'í* means 'a follower of the light'. Bahá'ís – 'the followers of the light' – are to be found widely scattered today in nearly every country of the world.

Detailed, authoritative accounts of the history of the Bahá'í Faith exist, and the particular circumstances under which Bahá'í Golden Rule statements were made are usually known.* Also, the Bahá'í teachings exist in their original form, an advantage in establishing their authenticity not always enjoyed among the older religions.

The early 1800s was a period of religious expectancy in many parts of the world. For example, many Christians were expecting the return of Christ around the years 1843–5.[3] It was commonly believed that two Manifestations would appear at about that time: 'in the Gospel the return of Christ and Elijah is promised.'[4]

Born on 20 October 1819 in the city of Shíráz, Persia, Siyyid 'Alí-Muhammad declared himself to be the Báb ('Gate'), a new Manifestation of God, on 23 May 1844.

This illustrious soul arose with such power that he shook the supports of the religion, of the morals, the conditions, the habits, and the customs of Persia, and instituted new rules, new laws, and a new religion.[5]

Opposition to the Báb and the followers of his faith was very severe, being incited by powerful religious and government leaders. About 20,000 Bábí men, women and children were martyred, often with unspeakable cruelty.

---

* See, for example, Shoghi Effendi, *God Passes By*, and the several volumes by Adib Taherzadeh, *The Revelation of Bahá'u'lláh*.

The Báb himself was subjected to innumerable indignities, including imprisonment first in the castle of Máh-Kú and next in the castle of Chihríq. The warden of Chihríq had been given strict instructions not to allow anyone to enter into the presence of the Báb. But from the beginning, the love of the Báb penetrated the warden's heart and transformed his being. No one, then, was refused admittance to the castle. The provisions required for the Báb were purchased in a nearby town and transported to his prison.

One day the Báb asked that some honey be purchased for Him. The price at which it had been bought seemed to Him exorbitant. He refused it and said: 'Honey of a superior quality could no doubt have been purchased at a lower price. I who am your example have been a merchant by profession. It behoves you in all your transactions to follow in My way. You must neither defraud your neighbour nor allow him to defraud you. Such was the way of your Master. The shrewdest and ablest of men were unable to deceive Him, nor did He on His part choose to act ungenerously towards the meanest and most helpless of creatures.' He insisted that the attendant who had made that purchase should return and bring back to Him a honey superior in quality and cheaper in price.[6]

After years of suffering and imprisonment, the Báb was martyred on 9 July 1850 in the city of Tabriz under some of the most extraordinary and astounding circumstances to be found in the pages of history.[7]

Although the writings of the Báb (the greatest being the Persian *Bayán*) were vast and varied, many of them were lost in the tumult. Most of the voluminous writings that remain have not been translated into English.*

The Báb had a twofold mission: to call humanity to God and to foretell and prepare the way for the appearance of another Manifestation of God whose message he clearly

---

* Some of the writings of the Báb are now available in *Selections from the Writings of the Báb* (Haifa: Bahá'í World Centre, 1976).

indicated would be much greater than his own. This was Bahá'u'lláh. Through his writings and other means, the Báb prepared many people to accept Bahá'u'lláh when he was to appear. That this effort was successful is illustrated by the fact that over 99% of the Bábís eventually became Bahá'ís.

One example in the Báb's writings of the Golden Rule is found in the *Kitáb-i-Asmá* (The Book of Names) ('Him Whom God shall make manifest' is commonly understood to refer to Bahá'u'lláh.):

O ye that are invested with the Bayán! Denounce ye not one another, ere the Day-Star of ancient eternity shineth forth above the horizon of His sublimity. We have created you from one tree and have caused you to be as the leaves and fruit of the same tree, that haply ye may become a source of comfort to one another. Regard ye not others save as ye regard your own selves, that no feeling of aversion may prevail amongst you so as to shut you out from Him Whom God shall make manifest on the Day of Resurrection. It behooveth you all to be one indivisible people; thus should ye return unto Him Whom God shall make manifest.[8]

Mírzá Ḥusayn 'Alí Núrí, who later adopted the name Bahá'u'lláh (the 'Glory of God' or the 'Light of God') was born on 12 November, 1817, in Teheran, the capital of Persia, the son of a favoured minister of the Crown. Society in Persia at that time was noted for its religious fanaticism, ignorance, corruption and degradation of morals. After the declaration of the Báb, Bahá'u'lláh accepted the new faith and became extremely active in its promulgation. In 1852, after the commitment of a deplorable act by two young, irresponsible Bábís, Bahá'u'lláh, who had nothing to do with the act, was cast into a terrible underground prison in Teheran with forty Bábís, a prison that also held murderers and highwaymen. During the four months of his intense suffering in this horrible place, Bahá'u'lláh had the first intimation that he was a Manifestation of God.

After being released, Bahá'u'lláh was exiled from Persia in 1853 by the authorities, never to return. Bahá'u'lláh went to Iraq and lived for some years in Baghdad. There he revealed a number of important works, including *The Hidden Words*, the *Kitáb-i-Íqán* (Book of Certitude), *The Seven Valleys* and *The Four Valleys*. Evidence of his rising influence led those who opposed him to make him leave Iraq in 1863 for the capital of the Ottoman Empire, Constantinople (now known as Istanbul). But before taking the long journey to Constantinople, Bahá'u'lláh openly declared himself to be the Manifestation of God the Báb had foretold.

Bahá'u'lláh and his companions stayed in Constantinople for about three months, after which they were moved to Adrianople. During the years spent in that city, Bahá'u'lláh took yet another significant step by beginning to write a series of highly important letters. He

. . . proclaimed in clear and unmistakable language, to the kings and rulers of the world, to its religious leaders, and to mankind in general that the long-promised age of world peace and brotherhood had at last dawned and that He Himself was the Bearer of the new message and power from God which would transform the prevailing system of antagonism and enmity between men and create the spirit and form of the destined world order.[9]

The most momentous Tablet (letter) Bahá'u'lláh wrote in the course of this proclamation was the *Súriy-i-Múlúk* (Súrih of Kings). But the messages to specific leaders of the world either met with derision or were ignored (the one exception being Queen Victoria), and in one instance the youthful bearer of the message was tortured for three days and then killed. When the kings and rulers failed to respond to his call, Bahá'u'lláh sorrowfully prophesied that mankind would undergo great sufferings until it finally accepted the guidance of God.

In 1868 the last exile of Bahá'u'lláh took place, to the foul prison-city of 'Akká in what is now Israel but which at that time was in the Ottoman Empire. During this last period of his life until his death on 29 May 1892 Bahá'u'lláh revealed many significant works, the most important being the *Kitáb-i-Aqdas* (The Book of Laws). Additional important works revealed at this time include the *Epistle to the Son of the Wolf* and the *Kalimát-i-Firdawsíyyih* (Words of Paradise).

The writings of Bahá'u'lláh, in modern Persian, classical Persian and Arabic, are voluminous and various, including poems, epigrams, prayers, exhortations, expositions, counsels and laws, and are most beautiful, powerful and eloquent. Bahá'u'lláh declared:

All praise be to the one true God – exalted be His glory – inasmuch as He hath, through the Pen of the Most High, unlocked the doors of men's hearts. Every verse which this Pen hath revealed is a bright and shining portal that discloseth the glories of a saintly and pious life, of pure and stainless deeds.[10]

Bahá'ís believe that Bahá'u'lláh is the latest – but not the last – Manifestation of God to appear and that his revelation is particularly intensive. He has been vividly described by the Guardian of the Bahá'í Faith, Shoghi Effendi, as

. . . the Organizer of the entire planet . . . the Unifier of the children of men . . . the Establisher of the Most Great Peace . . . the Proclaimer of the coming of age of the entire human race . . . the Creator of a new World Order . . . the Inspirer and Founder of a world civilization.[11]

The sacred texts of the Bahá'í Faith consist, then, in the writings of the Báb and Bahá'u'lláh (considered by the Bahá'ís to be Manifestations of God) and in the writings and talks of 'Abdu'l-Bahá (Servant of Bahá), the eldest son of Bahá'u'lláh who was designated by his father as the authoritative interpreter of his word and the centre of his covenant. 'Abdu'l-Bahá – known to many as 'The Master' – is thus considered to be not a Manifestation of God but rather the perfect man: the exemplar of Bahá'í teaching, the embodiment of every Bahá'í ideal and virtue.[12]

To discuss morality and ethics from a Bahá'í viewpoint is a far from easy task. To the writer's knowledge, no systematic treatment of ethics and morality from the Bahá'í teachings exists. The Bahá'í holy writings, which are voluminous as well as highly varied in content, are full of statements of moral and ethical significance. Shoghi Effendi stated that 'Every other word of Bahá'u'lláh's and 'Abdu'l-Baha's Writings is a preachment on moral and ethical conduct.'[13]

One writer esteemed by Bahá'ís, referring to the ethical teachings of Bahá'u'lláh, provides a valuable introduction to this subject:

The teachings of Bahá'u'lláh regarding personal conduct reaffirm many teachings of earlier Manifestations of God, but in reaffirming them, He renews their creative force and gives mankind a deeper insight into their true meaning. His system is not a mere synthesis of the ethical teachings of former Messengers of God; Bahá'u'lláh uncovers afresh the springs of righteousness and illumines the eyes of men with the light of Divine Guidance.

To some degree, all the teachings of Bahá'u'lláh influence personal conduct; for example, those on the Oneness of Mankind require Bahá'ís to adopt an attitude towards their fellow-men affecting every human relationship.[14]

The following treatment of Bahá'í morality and ethics within the framework of some important Bahá'í teachings must be regarded as sketchy, far from exhaustive, influenced by the demands of our subject and subject to the limitations of the understanding of the present writer.

However, it will provide us with a general context within which some very important issues related to reciprocity and the Golden Rule can be discussed from the Bahá'í view.

We may begin with the Bahá'í understanding of the nature of reality. 'Abdu'l Bahá explained, 'Know that the conditions of existence are limited to the conditions of servitude, of prophethood, and of Deity . . .'[15] The nature of these 'three worlds' was explained by a highly respected Bahá'í writer:

There are three well-defined, well-demarcated worlds or spheres, separate and distinct, yet linked and indissolubly bound: the world of God (the world of the Creator); the world of *logos* (the world of Manifestation); and the world of man (the world of the created). The world of Manifestation links the world of God with the world of man; and it is God, not man, Who determines Who that link shall be.[16]

At the very core of Bahá'í belief is the affirmation of the existence of God. But the essence of God is far, far beyond the understanding of man. We know God by His attributes, signs, names and perfections: God is Love, God is the All-Knowing, God is the All-Merciful, etc. But this knowledge is limited, while the attributes, names, perfections and signs of God are limitless. 'As the divine entity is eternal, the divine attributes are coexistent, coeternal.'[17] Bahá'u'lláh explained:

The virtues and attributes pertaining unto God are all evident and manifest, and have been mentioned and described in all the heavenly Books. Among them are trustworthiness, truthfulness, purity of heart while communing with God, forbearance, resignation to whatever the Almighty hath decreed, contentment with the things His Will hath provided, patience nay thankfulness in the midst of tribulation, and complete reliance, in all circumstances, upon Him. These rank, according to the estimate of God, among the highest and most laudable of all acts.[18]

The centre and source of all virtues is God. Man can manifest divine attributes and can emulate God. 'Abdu'l-Bahá stated, 'If his morals become spiritual in character, his aspirations heavenly and his actions conformable to the will of God, man has attained the image and likeness of his Creator . . .'[19] This is achieved through divine education. Also, 'God hath created all humankind in His own image, after His own likeness. That is, men and women alike are the revealers of His names and attributes . . .'[20]

Man possesses the potentiality to reflect the Divine nature, but he can also allow his lower nature to predominate.

In man there are two natures: his spiritual or higher nature and his material or lower nature. In one he approaches God, in the other he lives for the world alone. Signs of both these natures are to be found in men. In his material aspect he expresses untruth, cruelty and injustice; all these are the outcome of his lower nature. The attributes of his Divine nature are shown forth in love, mercy, kindness, truth and justice, one and all being expressions of his higher nature. Every good habit, every noble quality belongs to man's spiritual nature, whereas all his imperfections and sinful actions are born of his material nature. If a man's Divine nature dominates his human nature, we have a saint.[21]

Man can thus acquire divine virtues and can voluntarily discontinue vices.

We may ask: Would not the practice of the Golden Rule in one's conduct towards others be a means for a person to develop his spiritual, higher nature? Is it not a 'good habit'? Certainly, as we have already noted and shall explore again later, the Rule is inseparably linked to the divine attributes of love and justice, which, from a Bahá'í view, are expressions of man's higher, spiritual nature.

The Holy Spirit is also fundamental in Bahá'í moral and ethical teachings. 'This Holy Spirit is the mediator between God and His creatures.'[22] 'The Holy Spirit it is which, through the mediation of the Prophets of God, teaches spiritual virtues to man and enables him to attain Eternal Life.'[23]

As has been discussed in previous chapters, the principle of reciprocity is indissolubly linked with our understanding of the Golden Rule. We saw how fundamental reciprocity is in human relationships, starting with the mother–child relationship, and how it is practised in all societies. We noted its links with love. We also explored its fundamental importance in specific Golden Rule statements. For instance, we found that the great sage K'ung-fu-tse, in answer to the query, 'Is there one word which may serve as a rule of practice for all one's life?' said, 'Is not RECI-PROCITY such a word? What you do not want done to yourself, do not do to others.' We discovered that the scope of the meaning of the word *reciprocity* is vast. We have obliquely touched upon the view that reciprocity may not only be practised between 'equals' – such as two or more human beings – but may also be practised by or may involve the participation of 'unequals' (for example, the relationship between man and God). Our understanding of the vast range of reciprocity and its fundamental impor-tance – which in turn throws light on the scope and immense importance of the Golden Rule – is greatly expanded through the writings of the Bahá'í Faith.

A prime example is the Bahá'í belief that the 'breaths of the Holy Spirit' are the cause of loving co-operation and reciprocity. 'Abdu'l-Bahá explained:

The Lord of mankind has caused His holy, divine Manifestations to come into the world. He has revealed His heavenly Books in order to establish spiritual brotherhood and through the power of the Holy Spirit has made it practicable for perfect fraternity to be realized among mankind . . .

It is evident, therefore, that the foundation of real brother-hood, the cause of loving cooperation and reciprocity and the source of real kindness and unselfish devotion is none other than the breaths of the Holy Spirit. Without this influence and animus it is impossible. We may be able to realize some degrees of fraternity through other motives, but these are limited associations and subject to change. When human brotherhood is founded upon the Holy Spirit, it is eternal, changeless, unlimited.[24]

Since, in the Bahá'í view, the Holy Spirit is the mediator between God and His creatures, it follows that the ultimate source of reciprocity and loving co-operation is the Almighty Himself. This, then, from the writer's view, would be the very foundation of reciprocity.

Another fundamental Bahá'í belief is that God is manifested and made known to man through His Manifestations, those great souls possessed of the Holy Spirit, the founders of the great religions of the world. They include Krishna, Abraham, Zarathustra, Moses, Buddha, Jesus Christ, Muḥammad, the Báb, Bahá'u'lláh and others. These Manifestations are inspired by God and their wills are absolutely submissive to His. Their knowledge is divine. Between them there is absolutely no rivalry. All the great revelators from God have contributed to the achievement of the purpose of religion.

. . . the purpose of religion is the acquisition of praiseworthy virtues, the betterment of morals, the spiritual development of mankind, the real life and divine bestowals. All the Prophets have been the promoters of these principles . . .[25]

In the Bahá'í view, the fundamental unity of the Manifestations of God is a reality, and they are unified in their aims and purposes. There is but one true religion and one God, by whatever name He may be called in the various faiths and tongues. Conflict between the followers of various faiths is deplorable from a Bahá'í view and must be avoided and prevented wherever possible. This would, it follows, include conflict over such issues as the superiority or inferiority of Golden Rule statements of Jesus Christ in comparison with those revealed by other Manifestations such as Zarathustra, Muḥammad and Bahá'u'lláh. A really sincere Bahá'í would act to promote greater consensus over such issues. A very important Bahá'í teaching is the ultimate reconciliation of the teachings of the Messengers of God. Bahá'u'lláh declared:

That the divers communions of the earth, and the manifold systems of religious belief, should never be allowed to foster the feelings of animosity among men is, in this Day, of the essence of the Faith of God and His Religion. These principles and laws, these firmly-established and mighty systems, have procceded from one Source, and are rays of one Light. That they differ one from another is to be attributed to the varying requirements of the ages in which they were promulgated.[26]

We may, therefore, surmise also that, in the last analysis, as in the case of reciprocity, the ultimate Source of the Golden Rule is the Almighty Himself through the Holy Spirit and the Manifestations, and that any differences between its various formulations as brought by the Manifestations may be attributed to the varying conditions in different societies and at different times. But these formulations have one source. A careful, prayerful study and practise of the Golden Rule should help break down 'the feelings of animosity among men'. Is it our desire for ourselves and all others to reciprocate discord for discord?

Another fundamental moral and ethical teaching of the Bahá'í Faith is the elimination of prejudice. The Manifestations and the divine religions have appeared so that prejudice may become a thing of the past and be replaced by love, co-operation and reciprocity. The present writer surmises that perhaps this could help explain why the Golden Rule is so widespread among the religions of the world. If we ponder about the matter, we can discover how an understanding and practice of the Rule can be a most powerful means of destroying prejudices of religion, race, tribe, nation and class. If a person were sincerely to practice the Rule in his life, he would think twice before speaking or acting in any derogatory manner towards, for example, a person of another religion because of any alleged religious differences. 'Abdu'l-Bahá explained:

One of the forms of prejudice which afflict the world of mankind is religious bigotry and fanaticism. When this hatred burns in human hearts, it becomes the cause of revolution, destruction, abasement of humankind and deprivation of the mercy of God. For the holy Manifestations and divine Founders of religion Themselves were completely unified in love and agreement, whereas Their followers are characterized by bitter antagonism and attitudes of hostility toward each other. God has desired for mankind the effulgence of love, but through blindness and misapprehension man has enveloped himself in veils of discord, strife and hatred. The supreme need of humanity is cooperation and reciprocity. The stronger the ties of fellowship and solidarity amongst men, the greater will be the power of constructiveness and accomplishment in all the planes of human activity. Without cooperation and reciprocal attitude the individual member of human society remains self-centered, uninspired by altruistic purposes, limited and solitary in development like the animal and plant organisms of the lower kingdoms.[27]

(The full text of the above statement may be found in the Appendix.) The writer has observed that a person who begins to seriously understand and practise the Golden Rule in his life will most probably notice how he is gradually drawn away from self-centredness and towards altruism. He can become more sympathetic and more careful in his conduct towards others as he mentally 'puts himself in their place' and can begin to appreciate, albeit to a limited extent, their desires, sufferings and frustrations, and what might be best in life for both *himself* and *them*. He can become more deeply concerned that, through his own conduct in following the Rule, he can become an instrument through which others may be helped to lead a better life, closer to God.

A closely related Bahá'í teaching is that the unity of the human race is the goal towards which all peoples, often unknowingly, are moving. In time, as a fundamental aspect of the achievement of that unity, the universal recognition of one God and allegiance to one common Revelation will become a reality.[28]

. . . if material civilization shall become organized in conjunction with divine civilization, if the man of moral integrity and intellectual acumen shall unite for human betterment and uplift with the man of spiritual capacity, the happiness and progress of the human race will be assured. All the nations of the world will then be closely related and companionable, and the religions will merge into one, for the divine reality within them all is one reality.[29]

The achievement of unity and love is fundamental to religion. 'The essence of all religions is the Love of God, and it is the foundation of all the sacred teachings.'[30] Little wonder, then, that love is so closely interlinked with the Golden Rule! This unity and love has been promulgated not only by the Manifestations, but by others too. 'Abdu'l-Bahá declared:

Consider how the Prophets Who have been sent, the great souls who have appeared and the sages who have arisen in the world have exhorted mankind to unity and love. This has been the essence of their mission and teaching. This has been the goal of their guidance and message. The Prophets, saints, seers and philosophers have sacrificed their lives in order to establish these principles and teachings amongst men.[31]

Thus, from this point of view we may say that mankind

should deeply appreciate not only the contributions of all the Manifestations towards the achievement of unity and love, but also those of other distinguished figures such as the poet Kabír and the sage Lao-Tse – contributions whose essential elements included their teachings of the Golden Rule.

But this one religion, a religion that upholds the 'self-same exalted standard of individual conduct', is renewed from time to time through the successive Manifestations. And the signs of the need for renewal are evident in our age. Shoghi Effendi asserted:

Who, contemplating the helplessness, the fears, and miseries of humanity in this day, can any longer question the necessity for a fresh revelation of the quickening power of God's redemptive love and guidance? Who, witnessing on one hand the stupendous advance achieved in the realm of human knowledge, of power, of skill and inventiveness, and viewing on the other the unprecedented character of the sufferings that afflict, and the dangers that beset, present-day society, can be so blind as to doubt that the hour has at last struck for the advent of a new Revelation, for a re-statement of the Divine Purpose, and for the consequent revival of those spiritual forces that have, at fixed intervals, rehabilitated the fortunes of human society? Does not the very operation of the world-unifying forces that are at work in this age necessitate that He who is the Bearer of the Message of God in this day [Bahá'u'lláh] should not only reaffirm that self-same exalted standard of individual conduct inculcated by the Prophets gone before Him, but embody in His appeal, to all governments and peoples, the essentials of that social code, that Divine Economy, which must guide humanity's concerted efforts in establishing that all-embracing federation which is to signalize the advent of the Kingdom of God on this earth?[32]

In the Bahá'í view, what the world needs most desperately is love and unity, and it is for that very purpose that Bahá'u'lláh has come. 'Abdu'l-Bahá explained:

The essence of Bahá'u'lláh's Teaching is all-embracing love, for love includeth every excellence of humankind. It causeth every soul to go forward. It bestoweth on each one, for a heritage, immortal life. Ere long shalt thou bear witness that His celestial Teachings, the very glory of reality itself, shall light up the skies of the world.[33]

Among many other teachings aimed at the achievement of love and the unity of mankind, Bahá'u'lláh has taught that there must be a unity of the nations in a world commonwealth and the establishment of a new world order. To go into this matter in detail would divert us from our purpose.* But the reader will recall that the immorality of nations in their relationships with each other has been a cause of immense suffering and, indeed, threatens the very existence of the whole human race. We have also seen where, in the words of one prominent thinker, the Golden Rule for nations in their mutual intercourse seems to be, 'Do unto others as evilly as you can find an excuse for.' Morality in international relations is an important aspect of the Bahá'í teachings. With the achievement of spiritual reciprocity and love, international agreement can become a reality. Speaking of how Bahá'u'lláh appeared from the Orient, 'Abdu'l-Bahá explained:

[Bahá'u'lláh] established the foundation for international peace, caused the hearts of nations to be cemented together and conferred new life upon the various peoples of the East. Among those who have followed the teachings of Bahá'u'lláh no one says 'I am a Persian', 'I am a Turk', 'I am a Frenchman', or 'I am an Englishman'. No one says, 'I am a Muslim, upholding the only true religion', 'I am a Christian, loyal to my traditional and inherited beliefs', 'I am a Jew, following talmudic interpretations', or 'I am a Zoroastrian and opposed to all other religions'. On the contrary, all have been rescued from religious, racial,

* For an introduction to the Bahá'í view of the eventual achievement of world unity, a new world order and a world commonwealth see Shoghi Effendi, *The World Order of Bahá'u'lláh* (Wilmette, Illinois: Bahá'í Publishing Trust, 1955), pp. 202–6.

political and patriotic prejudices and are now associating in fellowship and love . . .

. . . it is necessary that we should cast aside all the prejudices of ignorance, discard superannuated beliefs in traditions of past ages and raise aloft the banner of international agreement. Let us cooperate in love and through spiritual reciprocity enjoy eternal happiness and peace.[34]

Thus we must be universal in our application of the Golden Rule towards others. Their nationality, race, religion, or whatever, must not be a barrier towards the achievement of this aim. National pride coupled with feelings of national superiority obviously involves the attitude that other nations and their peoples are inferior to your own. How can such an attitude be in the spirit of the Golden Rule?

In the chapter treating the subject of the Golden Rule in Christianity we have already discussed the Bahá'í approach to progressive revelation. Bahá'ís believe that the Bahá'í Revelation is one important, essential, and integral part of a process that has neither beginning nor end. Bahá'u'lláh declared in the *Kitáb-i-Aqdas*:

This is the changeless Faith of God, eternal in the past, eternal in the future. Let him that seeketh, attain it; and as to him that hath refused to seek it – verily, God is Self-Sufficient, above any need of His creatures.[35]

As we shall see later, the Golden Rule statements to be found in the Bahá'í Faith are harmonious with those found in the religions of the past. Nor is it surprising that a Bahá'í could foresee the possibility of the Golden Rule being given in future by a Manifestation or Manifestations of God. Bahá'u'lláh stated that the next Manifestation would appear after the expiration of a full thousand or thousands of years.

What amounts to a *staggering* new vision of the possible scope of reciprocity and the Golden Rule can be found in the teachings of the Bahá'í Faith about the universe and creation. For the endless process of divine revelation cannot be separated from the endless process of God's creation. The Báb declared:

The process of His creation hath had no beginning and can have no end, otherwise it would necessitate the cessation of His celestial grace. God hath raised up Prophets and revealed Books as numerous as the creatures of the world, and will continue to do so to everlasting.[36]

Bahá'u'lláh explained the purpose of God's creation:

Having created the world and all that liveth and moveth therein, He, through the direct operation of His unconstrained and sovereign Will, chose to confer upon man the unique distinction and capacity to know Him and to love Him – a capacity that must needs be regarded as the generating impulse and the primary purpose underlying the whole of creation.[37]

Indeed, the most basic purpose of man is to know and love God. This is an essential element of the moral and ethical teachings of the Bahá'í Faith.

Further, 'Abdu'l-Bahá explained:

. . . the names and attributes of the Divinity themselves require the existence of beings . . . Know that an educator without pupils cannot be imagined; a monarch without subjects could not exist; a master without scholars cannot be appointed; a creator without a creature is impossible; a provider without those provided for cannot be conceived; for all the divine names and attributes demand the existence of beings. If we could imagine a time when no beings existed, this imagination would be the denial of the Divinity of God . . . Therefore, as the Essence of Unity (that is the existence of God) is everlasting and eternal – that is to say, it has neither beginning nor end – it is certain that this world of existence, this endless universe, has neither beginning nor end.* Yes, it may be that one of the parts of the universe, one of the

---

* The belief that 'this world of existence, this endless universe has neither beginning nor end' is not commonly held among followers of Judaism, Christianity, Islám and other religions. Many statements of a scientific nature are found in Bahá'í literature.

globes, for example, may come into existence, or may be disin-
tegrated, but the other endless globes are still existing; the
universe would not be disordered nor destroyed. On the
contrary, existence is eternal and perpetual. As each globe has a
beginning, necessarily it has an end, because every composition,
collective or particular, must of necessity be decomposed . . .[38]

In answer to the question whether the physical world is
subject to any limitations, Bahá'u'lláh explained that '. . .
the comprehension of this matter dependeth upon the
observer himself. In one sense, it is limited: in another, it is
exalted above all limitations.'[39] The grandeur of the
universe and the number and nature of the creatures in it are
beyond our comprehension. But the words *universe* and
universal appear to have very deep meanings in the Bahá'í
writings. The Divinity '. . . has organized this infinite
universe in the most perfect form, and its innumerable
inhabitants with absolute system, strength, and perfection'.[40] Moreover, Bahá'u'lláh, long before modern
astronomy began to validate the existence of planets around
other stars besides our sun, explained that '. . . every fixed
star hath its own planets, and every planet its own creatures,
whose number no man can compute'.[41] We may ask: What
are these 'creatures'? Do they exist, depending on the conditions on each planet, on the mineral, vegetable, animal, and
human planes? Are there manlike creatures on other planets
in this infinite material universe? Many scientists now
believe that ours is not the only inhabited planet nor are we
the only highly intelligent beings in this material universe.
The writer vividly recalls during his college days attending
an outstanding public lecture given by one of the professors
of physics at the college on certain aspects of astronomy. He
cannot forget the professor's comment that since according
to man's knowledge at that time there were such a huge
number of stars in our universe, and so many of those stars
were likely to have planets on which conditions for life like

ours would exist, it was mathematically virtually impossible that beings like man did not exist somewhere in the universe! Now, we may again ask: If there are such intelligent beings – the term currently being used among many scientists is *humanoids* – have Manifestations of God appeared, are they appearing, and will they appear to them also? Time will reveal the answer to this most fascinating question. If the answer is *Yes*, claims of finality and uniqueness for revelations of the past on this earth that we have referred to previously will be delivered a severe blow! Bahá'u'lláh declared:

O people! I swear by the one true God! This is the Ocean out of which all seas have proceeded, and with which every one of them will ultimately be united. From Him all the Suns have been generated, and unto Him they will all return. Through His potency the Trees of Divine Revelation have yielded their fruits, every one of which hath been sent down in the form of a Prophet, bearing a Message to God's creatures in each of the worlds whose number God, alone, in His all-encompassing Knowledge, can reckon.[42]

Further, we may ask: If Manifestations of God appear throughout this limitless universe, do they, too, teach the equivalent of the Golden Rule? Again, time will reveal at least a partial answer to this other most fascinating question. Can it be that, from this perspective, our understanding of the Rule is in its infancy?

'Abdu'l-Bahá declared, ' . . . all the members and parts of the universe are very strongly linked together in that limitless space, and this connection produceth a reciprocity of material effects.'[43] Thus we see again, from a Bahá'í view, another dimension of the fundamental importance and significance of reciprocity. In fact, the parts of this infinite universe not only have their members and elements connected with one another but also influence one another spiritually and materially, although by existing rules and present-day science these cannot be discovered.[44]

In the Bahá'í teachings the assertion is made that there are innumerable worlds of God, that this material world is only one part of God's infinite creation, that the creation of God embraces creatures apart from these creatures. Not only that:

The worlds of God are in perfect harmony and correspondence one with another. Each world in this limitless universe is, as it were, a mirror reflecting the history and nature of all the rest. The physical universe is, likewise, in perfect correspondence with the spiritual or divine realm. The world of matter is an outer expression or facsimile of the inner kingdom of spirit.[45]

All created things are connected one to another in a complete and perfect relationship.[46]

In a talk on the subject of the modification of species in *Some Answered Questions*, 'Abdu'l-Bahá explained that

. . . all beings are connected together like a chain; and reciprocal help, assistance, and interaction belonging to the properties of things are the causes of the existence, development and growth of created beings. It is confirmed through evidences and proofs that every being universally acts upon other beings, either absolutely or through association.[47]

Thus, from this point of view, reciprocity is a universal phenomenon that is indispensable for the existence, growth and development of created beings, not merely, as we have noted previously, for man on this tiny planet! But, from the present writer's view, reciprocal relationships between a man and another man are not in every sense identical to those, for instance, between a man and a plant. And, as we shall investigate in the next chapter, reciprocal relationships can exist not only between beings on this material level of existence but between souls in this world and the next.

Our sampling of a few of the Bahá'í teachings related to

our theme leads us to a return to, perhaps, the most important issue facing each of us: the very purpose of our being. The basic purpose of man is to know and love God. This love and this knowledge are to be sought because they are needed not only for this life but also in the life to come. The purpose of life may also be expressed as the acquisition of the qualities, characteristics and attributes needed in the world to which we shall pass after leaving this earthly existence. In the words of 'Abdu'l-Bahá:

What is he in need of in the Kingdom which transcends the life and limitation of this mortal sphere? That world beyond is a world of sanctity and radiance; therefore it is necessary that in this world he should acquire these divine attributes. In that world there is need of spirituality, faith, assurance, the knowledge and love of God. These he must attain in this world so that after his ascension from the earthly to the heavenly Kingdom he shall find all that is needful in that life eternal ready for him.[48]

Surely, an essential element in the development of a person's spirituality is an ever-improving conduct towards others based on such things as love, reciprocity, and the Golden Rule. The Golden Rule has, we therefore think, an important role to play in a man's preparation for the next life.

Finally, it seems appropriate for us to briefly view, from a Bahá'í viewpoint, the crucial problem of carrying through high ideals to action. This fundamental issue has not only deeply concerned religionists but educationalists and psychologists as well. On this point 'Abdu'l-Bahá enjoined:

The wrong in the world continues to exist just because people talk only of their ideals, and do not strive to put them into practice. If actions took the place of words, the world's misery would very soon be changed into comfort.

A man who does great good, and talks not of it, is on the way to perfection.

The man who has accomplished a small good and magnifies it in his speech is worth very little.[49]

Moral educators today are aware that a person cannot practise the Golden Rule unless he is not only aware of it but has some understanding of its application to concrete situations and then carries through that understanding in action. (And – we might add – without boasting about it!)

16

Some Golden Rule Statements in the Bahá'í Writings

The Hidden Words is considered to be one of the brightest jewels in the revelation of Bahá'u'lláh. Revealed partly in Persian and partly in Arabic in about the year AD 1858 during Bahá'u'lláh's sojourn in Baghdad while he paced in meditation upon the banks of the River Tigris, *The Hidden Words* was originally known in the early days of the Bahá'í Faith as the 'Hidden Book of Fáṭimih'. This work is brief, containing fewer than eight thousand words. As with all great religious literature, it is inspiring, powerful, deep and penetrating. A Bahá'í writer has described it as '. . . a perfect guide-book for man on his journey to the spiritual worlds of God'.[1] From a Bahá'í view, the essence, the vital substance of religion is summed up in *The Hidden Words*. The significance of this book was indicated by Bahá'u'lláh himself in its opening passage and explained by Shoghi Effendi:

The significance of this dynamic spiritual leaven cast into the life of the world for the reorientation of the minds of men, the edification of their souls and the rectification of their conduct can best be judged by the description of its character given in the opening passage by its Author: 'This is that which hath descended from the Realm of Glory, uttered by the tongues of power and might, and revealed unto the Prophets of old. We have taken the inner essence thereof and clothed it in the garment of brevity, as a token of grace unto the righteous, that they may stand faithful unto the Covenant of God, may fulfill in their lives His trust, and in the realm of spirit obtain the gem of Divine virtue.'[2]

Any Golden Rule statement therein thus takes on a heightened significance from a Bahá'í view. The reader may also wish to bear in mind that the message Bahá'u'lláh brought to mankind ' . . . recognizes the divine origin and upholds the first principles of every Dispensation inaugurated by the prophets of the past, and stands inextricably interwoven with each one of them'.[3] 'Abdu'l-Bahá advised to 'read it [The Hidden Words] that you may understand the true foundations of religion and reflect upon the inspiration of the Messengers of God. It is light upon light.'[4] Shoghi Effendi explained that it stands pre-eminent among the ethical writings of Bahá'u'lláh.[5]

In the Arabic section of The Hidden Words there is a remarkable group of passages, the fourth of which contains a negative statement of the Rule:

O Son of Being!
How couldst thou forget thine own faults and busy thyself with the faults of others? Whoso doeth this is accursed of Me.

O Son of Man!
Breathe not the sins of others so long as thou art thyself a sinner. Shouldst thou transgress this command, accursed wouldst thou be, and to this I bear witness.

O Son of Spirit!
Know thou of a truth: He that biddeth men be just and himself committeth iniquity is not of Me, even though he bear My name!

O Son of Being!
Ascribe not to any soul that which thou wouldst not have ascribed to thee, and say not that which thou doest not. This is My command unto thee, do thou observe it.[6]

The potent words 'Ascribe not to any soul that which thou wouldst not have ascribed to thee' provide us with a fine illustration of how one religious teaching can provide deeper insight into other teachings and vice versa. These very words were cited by John E. Esslemont in his classic introduction to the Bahá'í Faith, *Bahá'u'lláh and the New Era*, in the section entitled 'The Sin-covering Eye.'[7] Although these words can be related to many other teachings, Esslemont, among other things, related them forcefully to the Bahá'í teaching that man is required to abstain from fault-finding. (Prohibitions against both backbiting and calumny are found in the *Kitáb-i-Aqdas*.)

The *Kitáb-i-Íqán* is the most important doctrinal work of Bahá'u'lláh that has been translated in full into English, again in authoritative form by Shoghi Effendi. As in the case of *The Hidden Words*, it was revealed during the period of Bahá'u'lláh's stay in Baghdad. The best available commentary on the book is from the pen of its translator:

Foremost among the priceless treasures cast forth from the billowing ocean of Bahá'u'lláh's Revelation ranks the Kitáb-i-Íqán (Book of Certitude), revealed within the space of two days and two nights, in the closing years of that period (1278 AH – 1862 AD). It was written in fulfillment of the prophecy of the Báb, who had specifically stated that the Promised One would complete the text of the unfinished Persian Bayán, and in reply to the questions addressed to Bahá'u'lláh by the as yet unconverted maternal uncle of the Báb . . . A model of Persian prose, . . . this Book, setting forth in outline the Grand Redemptive Scheme of God, occupies a position unequalled by any work in the entire range of Bahá'í literature, except the Kitáb-i-Aqdas, Bahá'u'lláh's Most Holy Book. Revealed on the eve of the declaration of His Mission, it proffered to mankind the '*Choice Sealed Wine*', whose seal is of '*musk*', and broke the '*seals*' of the '*Book*' referred to by Daniel, and disclosed the meaning of the '*words*' destined to remain '*closed up*' till the '*time of the end*'.[8]

In the *Kitáb-i-Íqán* we find ' . . . Bahá'u'lláh's masterly
exposition of the one unifying truth underlying all the
Revelations of the past . . . '[9] He also explains progressive
revelation, the doctrine that Prophets reveal teachings in
conformity with the capacity and needs of people, and those
difficulties of interpretation that have caused so much
discord and conflict among the great religions of the world.
Shoghi Effendi explained:

Well may it be claimed that of all the books revealed by the
Author of the Bahá'í Revelation, this Book alone, by sweeping
away the age-long barriers that have so insurmountably
separated the great religions of the world, has laid down a broad
and unassailable foundation for the complete and permanent
reconciliation of their followers.*[10]

Again, in the light of the above, the existence of a Golden
Rule statement in the *Kitáb-i-Íqán* is especially significant
from a Bahá'í view.

Among a number of subjects in the book, Bahá'u'lláh
' . . . enumerates the essential prerequisites for the attainment by every true seeker of the object of his quest . . . '[11]
Herein is to be found a negative version of the Rule (see the
Appendix for the whole text).

But, O my brother, when a true seeker determines to take the
step of search in the path leading to the knowledge of the Ancient
of Days, he must, before all else, cleanse and purify his heart,
which is the seat of the revelation of the inner mysteries of God,
from the obscuring dust of all acquired knowledge, and the
allusions of the embodiments of satanic fancy . . . He should not
hesitate to offer up his life for his Beloved, nor allow the censure
of the people to turn him away from the Truth. He should not
wish for others that which he doth not wish for himself, nor
promise that which he doth not fulfil . . .
    These are among the attributes of the exalted, and constitute

---

* For a further description of the book see Shoghi Effendi, *God Passes By* (Wilmette,
Illinois: Bahá'í Publishing Trust, 1965), p. 139.

the hall-mark of the spiritually-minded. They have already been mentioned in connection with the requirements of the wayfarers that tread the Path of Positive Knowledge. When the detached wayfarer and sincere seeker hath fulfilled these essential conditions, then and only then can he be called a true seeker. Whensoever he hath fulfilled the conditions implied in the verse: 'Whoso maketh efforts for Us',* he shall enjoy the blessing conferred by the words: 'In Our ways shall We assuredly guide him.'*[12]

Thus, following the Golden Rule is part of the path of a 'true seeker'.

Bahá'u'lláh and his companions arrived in Adrianople on 12 December 1863 and remained there for about four years. During his period of exile and suffering in that city, he revealed a very large number of Tablets (letters). His most momentous Tablet was the *Súriy-i-Múlúk* (Súrih of Kings), revealed in Arabic,

. . . in which He, for the first time, directs His words collectively to the entire company of the monarchs of East and West, and in which the Sultán of Turkey, and his ministers, the kings of Christendom, the French and Persian Ambassadors accredited to the Sublime Porte, the Muslim ecclesiastical leaders in Constantinople, its wise men and inhabitants, the people of Persia and the philosophers of the world are separately addressed . . .[13]

In this Tablet, Bahá'u'lláh sets forth his claims and station as a Manifestation of God in powerful and authoritative language. In one section, he directs his admonitions and counsels to the people of Constantinople. In fact, what he terms his 'best counsel' to them is a statement of the Golden Rule:

Beware that ye swell not with pride before God, and disdainfully reject His loved ones. Defer ye humbly to the faithful, they that have believed in God and in His signs, whose hearts witness to

* Qur'án 29:69.

His unity, whose tongues proclaim His oneness, and who speak not except by His leave. Thus do we exhort you with justice, and warn you with truth, lest perchance ye may be awakened.

Lay not on any soul a load which ye would not wish to be laid upon you, and desire not for any one the things ye would not desire for yourselves. This is My best counsel unto you, did ye but observe it.[14]

At the conclusion of this section he calls upon the people of Constantinople to give ear to his words, return to God, and repent.

On 31 August 1868 Bahá'u'lláh and his companions arrived at the prison–city of 'Akká in the Holy Land. Although his imprisonment was very severe at first, and his ordeals and tribulations were constant, his writings during this period until his passing on 29 May 1892 were voluminous. Among them were those that constitute the sequel to the proclamation of his mission while in Adrianople, particularly to the kings of the earth but also to others. One of the most significant of these Tablets is the one addressed to Queen Victoria. This Tablet contains words directed not only to the Queen herself but to rulers and kings in general. Included in these general counsels we find an admonition to follow the Golden Rule (in positive form) linked to warning to refrain from injustice:

O kings of the earth! We see you increasing every year your expenditures, and laying the burden thereof on your subjects. This, verily, is wholly and grossly unjust. Fear the sighs and tears of this Wronged One, and lay not excessive burdens on your peoples. Do not rob them to rear palaces for yourselves; nay rather choose for them that which ye choose for yourselves. Thus We unfold to your eyes that which profiteth you, if ye but perceive. Your people are your treasures. Beware lest your rule violate the commandments of God, and ye deliver your wards to the hands of the robber. By them ye rule, by their means ye subsist, by their aid ye conquer. Yet, how disdainfully ye look upon them! How strange, how very strange![15]

Although Bahá'u'lláh admonishes the kings and rulers for their wrongdoings, his teachings contain nothing that can be construed as a disparagement or repudiation of the institution of kingship. He extolled the conduct of just and fair-minded kings. Indeed, as a general principle Bahá'ís must be loyal to their respective governments and never engage in seditious activities. In the *Riḍván-u'l-'Adl*, Bahá'u'lláh also prophesied that kings would arise who would exemplify justice and practise the Golden Rule.

Erelong will God make manifest on earth kings who will recline on the couches of justice, and will rule amongst men even as they rule their own selves. They, indeed, are among the choicest of My creatures in the entire creation.[16]

Another noteworthy Tablet revealed during the time Bahá'u'lláh was a prisoner and exile in 'Akká was the *Kalimát-i-Firdawsíyyih* (Words of Paradise), described by Shoghi Effendi as among those Tablets that ' . . . must rank among the choicest fruits which His mind has yielded . . .'[17] As in the *Riḍván-u'l-'Adl*, the relationship between the Rule (again in positive form) and justice is highlighted:

The word of God which the Supreme Pen hath recorded on the *third leaf* of the Most Exalted Paradise is this: O son of man! If thine eyes be turned towards mercy, forsake the things that profit thee and cleave unto that which will profit mankind. And if thine eyes be turned towards justice, choose thou for thy neighbour that which thou choosest for thyself. Humility exalteth man to the heaven of glory and power, whilst pride abaseth him to the depths of wretchedness and degradation.[18]

We have already noted several instances of relationships between the Rule and law in religion. Around 1873, while in 'Akká, Bahá'u'lláh revealed his most momentous work,

the *Kitáb-i-Aqdas* (The Book of Laws), a book Bahá'ís
believe to be the charter of the future world civilisation.
Shoghi Effendi explained that the *Kitáb-i-Aqdas*

. . . stands out, by virtue of the principles it inculcates, the
administrative institutions it ordains and the function with which
it invests the appointed Successor* of its Author, unique and
incomparable among the world's sacred Scriptures . . .[19]

and that it

. . . not only preserves for posterity the basic laws and ordinances
on which the fabric of [Bahá'u'lláh's] future World Order must
rest, but ordains . . . the necessary institutions through which the
integrity and unity of His Faith can alone be safeguarded.[20]

Among these institutions is the House of Justice. The
Universal House of Justice is the supreme administrative
body of the Bahá'í Faith. Its basic functions are administrative and legislative. At present there are also many
National Spiritual Assemblies and very many Local
Spiritual Assemblies, institutions that will in time be
termed Secondary Houses of Justice and Local Houses of
Justice. These, along with the Universal House of Justice,
are elected bodies. Bahá'u'lláh enjoined in the *Kitáb-i-Aqdas*
(in this instance in positive form) that Houses of Justice
follow the Golden Rule:

The Lord hath ordained that in every city a House of Justice be
established wherein shall gather counsellors to the number of
Bahá [9], and should it exceed this number it does not matter . . .
It behoveth them to be the trusted ones of the Merciful among
men and to regard themselves as the guardians appointed of God
for all that dwell on earth. It is incumbent upon them to take
counsel together and to have regard for the interests of the
servants of God, for His sake, even as they regard their own
interests, and to choose that which is meet and seemly. Thus hath
the Lord your God commanded you. Beware lest ye put away

* 'Abdu'l-Bahá.

that which is clearly revealed in His Tablet. Fear God, O ye that perceive.[21]

We shall later investigate the relationship between justice and the Golden Rule in the Bahá'í writings in further detail.

Local Spiritual Assemblies consult with their communities every nineteen days at gatherings of the believers known as Nineteen Day Feasts. These have three parts: devotion, consultation and social activities. 'Abdu'l-Bahá explained that in the Nineteen Day Feasts 'the object is concord, that through this fellowship hearts may become perfectly united, and reciprocity and mutual helpfulness be established.'[22]

Prayer is very important in many religions – including the Bahá'í Faith – and very many prayers as well as writings on the subject of prayer were revealed by the Báb, Bahá'u'lláh and 'Abdu'l-Bahá. Bahá'ís have, in their Holy Writings, not only obligatory prayers but a great variety of other prayers for use at various times and for various purposes. The greatness of conception and depth of spirituality in these prayers are apparent even to the casual reader; how much more to the person who makes use of them regularly. In the collection of prayers and meditations translated by Shoghi Effendi and published under the title *Prayers and Meditations by Bahá'u'lláh*, we may find not only prayers for ordinary people to use but also prayers revealed by Bahá'u'lláh as an expression of his own communion with the Almighty. One of these refers to the opposition of some of his kindred and the ordeals he underwent at their hands; yet he expresses his deep love for them. In fact, it is well known historically that Bahá'u'lláh poured his love upon his adversaries – a noble example of universal unrequiting goodness.

Glorified art Thou, O Lord my God! Thou seest me dwelling in this prison-house that lieth behind the seas and the mountains, and knowest full well what I have endured for love of Thee and for the sake of Thy Cause . . .

I was, moreover, opposed by mine own kindred, although, as Thou knowest, they were dear to me and I had desired for them that which I had desired for mine own self. These are the ones who, when learning that I had been cast into prison, perpetrated against me what no man else on earth had perpetrated.

I entreat Thee, therefore, O my God, by Thy name by which Thou hast separated between truth and denial, to purify their hearts of all evil suggestions, and to enable them to draw nigh unto Him Who is the Day-Spring of Thy names and Thine attributes.[23]

Interestingly, here the Manifestation expresses an approximation of the Golden Rule in his relationship with men: '. . . I have desired for them that which I had desired for mine own self.' We recall that this same basic relationship was indicated between Zarathustra and others in the *Sad Dar*. Whether these statements are corollaries of the Rule because they involve relationships between what many would regard as 'unequals', or statements of the Rule itself, was discussed in the chapter on Zoroastrianism. In the Bahá'í writings the dual station – divine and human – of the Manifestations of God is upheld. Likewise, their utterances may be divided into two classes: those that purport to be the direct words of God Himself and those in which each Manifestation writes or speaks as a man who has been obliged by God to convey a message to his fellows.

As we have noted earlier, Bahá'ís believe that Bahá'u'lláh's eldest son, 'Abdu'l-Bahá, was not a Manifestation of God but a very great man. Bahá'u'lláh had appointed him as the only person to whom the Bahá'ís were to turn for guidance after his passing, as the unerring interpreter of his word. Thus we find the teachings and principles of Bahá'u'lláh explained and interpreted in detail in the writings and recorded talks of 'Abdu'l-Bahá.

One such subject is an endless one – life after death. The Bahá'í Faith firmly upholds belief in the continued existence of the soul after death, a belief that is held so commonly among the world's religions. The spiritual development achieved by a person in this world determines his station in the next, but the progress he can achieve in the next is without end. 'From the moment the soul leaves the body and arrives in the Heavenly World, its evolution is spiritual, and that evolution is: *The approaching unto God.*'[24] The condition of the soul after death is so wonderful that it is impossible to describe. Death is not to be feared, but is 'a messenger of joy'.

One important aspect of this boundless subject is the relationship between souls in this world and those that have departed for the other. Although they are in different worlds, no insurmountable barrier exists between them; on the contrary, they can assist and benefit each other.

Just as we have the power to pray in this world, we shall also possess the power to pray once we have made the inevitable journey to the next. 'Abdu'l-Bahá explained:

It is even possible that the condition of those who have died in sin and unbelief may become changed – that is to say, they may become the object of pardon through the bounty of God, not through His justice – for bounty is giving without desert, and justice is giving what is deserved. As we have power to pray for these souls here, so likewise we shall possess the same power in the other world, which is the Kingdom of God. Are not all the people in that world the creatures of God? Therefore, in that world also they can make progress. As here they can receive light by their supplications, there also they can plead for forgiveness and receive light through entreaties and supplications. Thus as souls in this world, through the help of the supplications, the entreaties and the prayers of the holy ones, can acquire development, so is it the same after death.[25]

In the collection of 'Abdu'l-Bahá's talks known as *'Abdu'l-*

Bahá in London, we find a most remarkable statement revealing what to many must be a new and unexpected dimension of the Golden Rule; its mutual practice in the form of prayer aids the progress of souls both in this world and the next!

Once a friend asked the Master ['Abdu'l-Bahá], 'How should one look forward to death?'

He replied, 'How does one look forward to the goal of any journey? With hope and with expectation. It is even so with the end of this earthly journey. In the next world, man will find himself freed from many of the disabilities under which he now suffers. Those who have passed on through death, have a sphere of their own. It is not removed from ours; their work, the work of the Kingdom, is ours; but it is sanctified from what we call 'time and place'. Time with us is measured by the sun. When there is no more sunrise, and no more sunset, that kind of time does not exist for man. Those who have ascended have different attributes from those who are still on earth, yet there is no real separation.

'In prayer there is a mingling of station, a mingling of condition. Pray for them as they pray for you!'[26]

Further, we can do more to benefit the souls of the departed than just pray for them. In the words of 'Abdu'l-Bahá:

The progress of man's spirit in the divine world, after the severance of its connection with the body of dust, is through the bounty and grace of the Lord alone, or through the intercession and the sincere prayers of other human souls, or through the charities and important good works which are performed in its name.[27]

A collection of 'Abdu'l-Bahá's talks given chiefly in Paris in 1912–13 includes a series on eleven principles of the Bahá'í Faith. The ninth talk in this series is on the non-interference of religion with politics. Here he gives two Golden Rule statements in positive form, the second illustrating the principle of universal unrequiting goodness, within a thought-provoking exposition of the subject of justice.

Oh, friends of God, be living examples of justice! So that by the Mercy of God, the world may see in your actions that you manifest the attributes of justice and mercy.

Justice is not limited, it is a universal quality. Its operation must be carried out in all classes, from the highest to the lowest. Justice must be sacred, and the rights of all the people must be considered. Desire for others only that which you desire for yourselves. Then shall we rejoice in the Sun of Justice, which shines from the Horizon of God.

Each man has been placed in a post of honour, which he must not desert. A humble workman who commits an injustice is as much to blame as a renowned tyrant. Thus we all have our choice between justice and injustice.

I hope that each one of you will become just, and direct your thoughts towards the unity of mankind; that you will never harm your neighbours nor speak ill of any one; that you will respect the rights of all men, and be more concerned for the interests of others than for your own. Thus will you become torches of Divine justice, acting in accordance with the Teaching of Bahá'u'lláh, who, during His life, bore innumerable trials and persecutions in order to show forth to the world of mankind the virtues of the World of Divinity, making it possible for you to realize the supremacy of the spirit, and to rejoice in the Justice of God.[28]

Obviously, then, the relationship of justice to the Golden Rule is given great emphasis in the Bahá'í writings, as is made clear in several statements from Bahá'u'lláh and 'Abdu'l-Bahá. Justice is a virtue widely lauded in the world's religions, while links exist between justice and reciprocity. The relationship between justice and the Rule has been recognised and investigated by various scholars. The crucial importance of the Rule in the exercise of justice was explained by Marcus G. Singer, who probably had Jesus Christ's statements of the Rule in mind.

. . . The Golden Rule formulates a fundamental requirement of justice, that everyone's conduct must be judged by the same standards, and that no one has, in general, any warranted claim to a special or privileged position. It is therefore at the basis of the Principle of Justice, that what is right or wrong for one person must be right or wrong for any similar person in similar circumstances. Stated differently but equivalently: What is right for one person cannot be wrong for another, unless there is some relevant difference in their natures or circumstances.[29]

The present writer would add that the Rule is an excellent guideline and can be relied upon in typical cases. He has found this to be true in his own life. Although relevant differences in the natures of people or circumstances do certainly exist and should be taken into account at times in the exercise of justice and the Golden Rule (for example, one would not always exercise the Rule in relationships with a dangerous, mentally ill mass-murderer in the same manner as with the vast majority of 'normal' people), one must often exercise great care in determining what those relevant differences and circumstances are. To a Bahá'í, other Bahá'í principles such as the elimination of prejudices based on race, tribe, religion, nationality, class, etc. would influence his thoughts, words, and actions in the exercise of justice and the Rule, and he would *not* regard, for example, differences in race only as some sort of excuse for not practising the Rule in one's relationships with other people. Unfortunately today very many people in the world unconsciously or consciously still practise such discrimination, a discrimination that must eventually, from a Bahá'í view, break down. Educating the peoples of the world more effectively about the Golden Rule will very probably play an important part in this process. We shall return later to consideration of some issues in modern education and the teaching and learning of the Rule.

We have already seen how the great sage Lao-Tse was

one of the early teachers of what is termed the principle of universal unrequiting goodness and have touched upon this issue and given examples of it in practice in various parts of this book. If justice requires that a man choose for others what he chooses for himself, then the principle of universal unrequiting goodness requires him to become even more altruistic, to help others regardless of himself and to return good for evil. Modern educationalists and psychologists regard the achievement of such altruism as an indication of a very high level of moral development.

Examples of the principle in the Bahá'í writings are so numerous that we cannot give them all in detail. Some examples have already been cited above; some additional ones follow.

In the *Kalimát-i-Firdawsíyyih* Bahá'u'lláh deals with the subject of charity and refers to an example of universal unrequiting goodness previously given in the chapter on Islám from the Qur'án, thus further demonstrating how, from a Bahá'í view, the revealed religions of the world complement and throw light on each other.

The word of God which the Supreme Pen hath recorded on the *tenth leaf* of the Most Exalted Paradise is the following:

. . . Charity is pleasing and praiseworthy in the sight of God and is regarded as a prince among goodly deeds. Consider ye and call to mind that which the All-Merciful hath revealed in the Qur'án: 'They prefer them before themselves, though poverty be their own lot. And with such as are preserved from their own covetousness shall it be well.'* Viewed in this light, the blessed utterance above is, in truth, the day-star of utterances. Blessed is he who preferreth his brother before himself. Verily, such a man is reckoned, by virtue of the Will of God, the All-Knowing, the All-Wise, with the people of Bahá who dwell in the Crimson Ark.[30]

In a similar vein, as included in a collection and translation

* Qur'án 59:9.

of Bahá'u'lláh's writings by Shoghi Effendi known as *Gleanings from the Writings of Bahá'u'lláh*, the principle of universal unrequiting goodness is enjoined upon the rich so that the poor of the earth may be relieved of some of their burdens and sufferings. An important Bahá'í teaching is the elimination of extremes of wealth and poverty, but it is preferable that the rich voluntarily and without coercion give of some of their substance to the poor. On the other hand, all must work and exert themselves to earn a livelihood. Bahá'u'lláh declared:

They who are possessed of riches, however, must have the utmost regard for the poor, for great is the honour destined by God for those poor who are steadfast in patience. By My life! There is no honour, except what God may please to bestow, that can compare to this honour. Great is the blessedness awaiting the poor that endure patiently and conceal their sufferings, and well is it with the rich who bestow their riches on the needy and prefer them before themselves.[31]

'Abdu'l-Bahá, being the chosen interpreter of the teachings of Bahá'u'lláh, expounded upon the subject of universal unrequiting goodness many times. We shall take several examples from *The Promulgation of Universal Peace*, a collection of talks given by 'Abdu'l-Bahá in the USA and Canada in 1912. Firstly, we see how the principle is inseparable from the compassion of God towards all and the practice of love and kindness towards others.

You must manifest complete love and affection toward all mankind. Do not exalt yourselves above others, but consider all as your equals, recognizing them as the servants of one God. Know that God is compassionate toward all; therefore, love all from the depths of your hearts, prefer all religionists before yourselves, be filled with love for every race, and be kind toward the people of all nationalities.[32]

We can contrast this injunction 'prefer all religionists before yourselves' to the innumerable examples of hatred, conflict and strife between followers of various religions and sects and between the forces of religion and irreligion so evident today. Bahá'ís are committed to work towards the reduction of this discord.

The principle of universal unrequiting goodness is lived by those who have been truly inspired by the teachings of Bahá'u'lláh.

Souls who have hearkened to His words and accepted His message live together today in complete fellowship and love. They even offer their lives for each other. They forego and renounce worldly possessions for one another, each preferring the other to himself. This has been due to the declaration and foundation of the oneness of the world of humanity.[33]

Indeed, practice of the principle by Bahá'ís is fundamental when teaching their Faith to others.

You must give the message through action and deed, not alone by word. Word must be conjoined with deed. You must love your friend better than yourself; yes, be willing to sacrifice yourself.[34]

In fact, the frequent examples of the Rule of Love and the principle of universal unrequiting goodness in the Bahá'í writings seem to the present writer to be a call, a summons, an exhortation to the whole human race not only to understand and practise the Rule on a higher level but to live up to a higher standard of morality than it has ever achieved in the past.

17

The Golden Rule and the Education of Mankind

The Bahá'í writings contain a very large number of references to moral and ethical education and it is impossible to treat them comprehensively here. One example that may serve as a starting-point for our discussion is from 'Abdu'l-Bahá, who explained that there are three types of education:

> . . . education is of various kinds. There is a training and development of the physical body which ensures strength and growth. There is intellectual education or mental training for which schools and colleges are founded. The third kind of education is that of the spirit. Through the breaths of the Holy Spirit man is uplifted into the world of moralities and illumined by the lights of divine bestowals. The moral world is only attained through the effulgence of the Sun of Reality and the quickening life of the divine spirit. For this reason the holy Manifestations of God appear in the human world.[1]

The teachings of the Manifestations, including their moral and ethical teachings, have a pervading effect. They spread widely among their followers and even influence people (including sages and philosophers) who do not even profess to follow their religions or, in some cases, have not even heard of them; this could be especially true of the Golden Rule statements originating from the Manifestations.

Moral education is regarded as fundamental not only in the Bahá'í teachings and among adherents of the Bahá'í Faith but also among the billions of followers of the world's other religions. The Universal House of Justice stated, 'The proper education of children is of vital importance to the progress of mankind, and the heart and essential foundation of all education is spiritual and moral training.'[2]

In the Bahá'í view, as well as the view of followers of many religions, moral and ethical education goes hand in hand with the teaching of religion. The schools of the world can contribute to the development of good character in children and youth through education in the principles of religion. In the words of Bahá'u'lláh found in the *Kalimát-i-Firdawsíyyih*:

The word of God which the Supreme Pen hath recorded on the *eighth leaf* of the Most Exalted Paradise is the following: Schools must first train the children in the principles of religion, so that the Promise and the Threat recorded in the Books of God may prevent them from the things forbidden and adorn them with the mantle of the commandments; but this in such a measure that it may not injure the children by resulting in ignorant fanaticism and bigotry.[3]

The present writer feels that there are likely to be several possible approaches to determining what these 'principles of religion' may be. One of these may be further investigation into what the religions of the world have in common. It has been shown in this book that the Golden Rule, although probably not universal in the form of statements among all the existing religions of the world, is very widespread, particularly among the world's major religions, and that reciprocity, which is so closely interlinked with the Rule, must exist in all human societies. Determination of the 'principles of religion' could very well also relate to an even more fundamental achievement: the ultimate reconciliation of the followers of the great religions of the world. Bahá'ís believe that fundamental guidelines towards the achievement of this aim are to be found in the sacred writings of their Faith such as the *Kitáb-i-Íqán* and that it is not a utopian dream. (Two hundred years ago virtually no one could have foreseen the present nature of the United Nations.) The present writer hopes that this book contributes in a modest way to the achievement of this aim by demonstrating, among other things, how commonly the Rule has been taught by the founders of the great religions of the world even if in some cases in the older religions there is some difficulty in proving that the Rule was among the original teachings of the founders, and by conveying something of the loving appreciation Bahá'ís have for all these founders and their contributions.

The book has also been written in the hope that some day the Golden Rule may be taught as one of many principles of religion in the schools of the world 'in such a measure that it may not injure the children by resulting in ignorant fanaticism and bigotry'. For the Bahá'í Faith also includes in its teachings one that the writer, being an educator, found at first thirty years ago to be a real challenge to his ideas of what education ought and ought not to include, but one that he discovers is now gradually becoming a reality: a universal curriculum. 'Abdu'l-Bahá linked the development of a universal curriculum in the future with ethics:

. . . education is essential, and all standards of training and teaching throughout the world of mankind should be brought into conformity and agreement; a universal curriculum should be established, and the basis of ethics be the same.[4]

The Golden Rule is a most fundamental ethical and moral teaching, possibly universal in its origins and scope. The writer foresees the possibility that its effective teaching and learning could very well constitute one of the lynchpins of moral and ethical education in a future universal curriculum. It is a challenging thought.

The Rule need not only be taught and learned in the schools of the world through formal classes on morals and ethics. In a work on school administration, the headmaster is advised to accomplish various educational aims in his school, including children 'working together as a team'.

Children cannot . . . learn to live or work in a social setting as a team before they have learned to respect the rights and feelings of others. As a miniature society, the school is, therefore, a model of the community. It should instil the golden rule of each child respecting the rights and feelings of others just as he would like them to respect his own rights and feelings.[5]

We can surely understand that the Rule can be learned in a wide variety of courses and activities in schools, such as in first aid and home science as well as on the playing field, in drama, in service projects, in co-operative research, etc. This would help reduce problems among children and with their teachers such as stealing, lying, cheating, making fun of each other, jealousies and prejudices based on such things as religion, colour and social standing. For example, a child who cheats on tests in school in order to get high marks often forgets that other children who are honest are getting relatively lower marks as a result. How would he like it if others in the class did the same thing to him? And what about the fears he has about being found out? And the problem he has later living with his own conscience? Educators could investigate the issue of inculcating the Rule and related teachings in the minds of children in such a manner as to greatly reduce such cheating.

The existence of the Bahá'í teachings referred to above and whatever speculations we may have about them also relate to man's evolving concept of the scope of education, about which we again find relevant statements in the Bahá'í writings. Most educationalists throughout the world now accept that education is carried out not only in schools but in the home, the community, through the media, etc. and is life-long, beginning, according to recent investigations, when the child is in the womb of its mother. A few thinkers, particularly religious thinkers in education such as the great Christian educationalist of the 1600s John Amos Comenius, had some inkling of its continuation after death. But there is at least one very clear statement by Shoghi Effendi through his secretary that spiritual education continues in the afterlife,[6] and if this is accepted, many other statements in the Bahá'í teachings about life and death can be understood better in relation to it. At any rate, the teaching and learning of the Golden Rule cannot be left merely as the concern of schoolmasters. Parents, the community and non-formal educational institutions are involved in the process, with parents playing a key role.

In fact, informal education and information referring to the Rule in everyday life take a wide, interesting and occasionally entertaining variety of forms. An African airline has placed this sign prominently in its booking and sales office in Nairobi, obviously for the attention of both its employees and customers:

Our oath of allegiance to our clients:
We hereby solemnly promise to treat each and every client, in each and all circumstances, in the manner in which we ourselves would wish to be treated. (Name of the airline)

Recently in the USA, T-shirts have been worn with the half-amusing, half-ominous words imprinted on them:

Do unto others before they do unto you.

One highly respected Bahá'í child psychologist, 'Alí-Akbar Furútan, has at several points indicated how essential the

Golden Rule is in education in the home.* Often parents, in their attempts to teach a moral point of view to their children, will try to explain it to them by getting them to put themselves into another person's place: 'How would you like it if he did that to you?' The parents can go a step further and explore with their children those standards or principles they might follow in their relations with others that they would like others to apply in their conduct towards them. An example that can serve as a stimulus to parents to take further action is found in *Mothers, Fathers and Children* in a section entitled 'Explaining Moral Subjects':

Educationalists are of the opinion that verbal counselling, including explanations of spiritual matters and statements of moral truths, will not have the desired effect of refining children's conduct and rectifying their behaviour unless they are combined with other educational principles. In spite of this, we cannot altogether disregard the importance of this kind of training. Mothers and fathers should make the most of this method, and arrange orderly and regular meetings. The parents should sit with their children and carry on the discussion at a friendly level . . .

For instance, one evening the parents may gather the children around and begin:

'Dear children, you all know that God has created us and all the creatures in the world. He is kind to all, shelters all, and provides for all, and is with us at all times. Whatever we do or say, and even whatever we think – He is aware of it, for one of His names is the All-Knowing. Since God desires good for us, and directs us only towards the right path, we must do our part, and sincerely try to obey His laws, and do whatever He has ordered us to do, and not do whatever He has forbidden, for our happiness and honour in this world, and in the world to come, depend only on this and on nothing else.

'The Prophets have said that whatever a person does not like, he should not wish for others. Whatever he does not want for

* See 'Alí-Akbar Furútan, *Mothers, Fathers and Children: Practical Advice to Parents* (Oxford: George Ronald, 1980), pp. 71–4, 256–9.

himself, he should not want for others. This is called "sympathis-
ing", and it means that we should put ourselves in the other
person's place so we can understand that whatever displeases us is
displeasing to him too.

'For instance, since we like other people to do nice things for us
and make us happy, we should do nice things for others too, and
not hurt their feelings. If your friend at school speaks harshly to
you or tears your note-book and breaks your pen, it is certain that
you won't be happy; therefore, you should not do such things to
your friend. And if your friend, because of a lack of understanding, does something that bothers you, then you should do
good to him in return and show him courtesy and friendship.
[This is a good example of universal unrequiting goodness.] In
this way, he will regret what he has done, will see how bad he has
been, and will stop treating you and other people in that way.'

We recall the words of the great sage Lao–Tse: 'To those
who are good (to me), I am good; and to those who are not
good (to me), I am also good; – and thus (all) get to be
good.' But the process of helping 'those who are not good
to me' to 'get to be good' is often not a simple one. It
requires motivation, understanding and persistent action
by the person trying to follow the principle, as well as
guidance from others such as parents. Furútan continues:

We should always be careful not to encroach on the life, the
substance or the honour of anyone. We should cherish other
people's lives and dignity as we do our own, so that we may
become worthy members of mankind. These characteristics are
called human perfections and moral virtues. Whoever does not
possess these traits remains far from fulfilling his potential as a
human being, and can even become worse than an animal, for
animals never commit deeds as bad as those by untrained people.[7]

Such a statement could be the basis for a good discussion
with the children of the principles involved, followed by
action that has been mutually agreed upon, and follow-up.

The reader will recall 'Abdu'l-Bahá's exhortation that good ideas must be carried through into action. All this sort of effort depends, of course, on the children's ages and levels of maturity.

The author and his wife have found, while attempting in a rudimentary way to teach the Rule and its practice in everyday life to their three boys (ages 12, 10 and 9) that apparent advantages exist in referring to and discussing various statements of the Rule rather than sticking to one, as this tends to open the door to a deeper and wider under-standing of its dimensions in life under various circumstances and may possibly contribute to its more effective practice (although we have no way of measuring this under our circumstances). This approach not only appears valuable in the education of children but in that of parents as well! Often, the opportunities for such education arise unsystematically and unexpectedly from events taking place in the home and neighbourhood.

An example will suffice. Our children had already been introduced to the Rule and had discussed it, usually in relation to problems they had experienced. Then one day the family was eating a meal together, and yet another vexing problem our boys faced in relationships with other children was brought up. (Raising children is a hard task!) We recalled and then discussed a statement of the Rule attri-buted to Buddha:

Is there a deed, Rahula, thou dost wish to do? Then bethink thee thus: 'Is this deed conducive to my own harm, or to others' harm, or to that of both?' Then is this a bad deed, entailing suffering. Such a deed must thou surely not do.

Among other things, we saw clearly how important it is *to think carefully first* about the effects upon yourself, another person or both before acting so that suffering does not result, although one son piped up, 'Sometimes you don't have time to think!' The reply was that we should try to take the time to do so whenever we are able.

In the modern world, many psychologists and educationalists have been deeply concerned with the Golden Rule within the context of moral education and moral development. We are not concerned here with the fine points and controversies that arise among the experts. But generally speaking it may be said that the Golden Rule as understood and practised by children and youth, and its relationship to the development of such things as justice, equity, reciprocity, love, and 'moral autonomy' has been investigated by various psychologists. (Such studies have typically omitted adults.) Perhaps the greatest of these investigators in recent years was Jean Piaget, whose classic work, *The Moral Judgment of the Child*, has constituted a major contribution in this field, with all subsequent studies being indebted to him in some sense. Such efforts should, we think, be intensified on a global scale.

That the Golden Rule is often regarded as fundamental in moral education is undoubted. Singer wrote, 'The Golden Rule, in fact, is an instrument of moral education, and the most effective one that I know of.'[8]

An appropriate means of ending our treatment of this important subject is to ponder a statement of the Rule from one of the books of Judaism, the *Tobit*:

Take heed to thyself, my child, in all thy works; and be discreet in all thy behaviour. And what thou thyself hatest, do to no man.[9]

18

The Fundamental Importance of the Golden Rule to Man

As we have seen, the Golden Rule existed long before the term 'Golden Rule' became known. The poet wrote, 'No man is an island' – man has never been able to exist by himself. In one sense, the Rule is an expression of certain aspects of reciprocity in relationships that are inextricably linked with love, justice, charity and other virtues. This reciprocity appears to be universal, ancient, permanent and essential. Evidence exists that reciprocity is practised in all societies in some form, so fundamental is it in human relationships. Yet the term 'Golden Rule' falls short of expressing the full scope and depth of the topic we have attempted to treat in this study. There is much more to it than the deceptively simple words 'Do unto others as you would have them do unto you'. Nevertheless, a simple man could progress greatly towards becoming a saint if he were to exemplify these few words and relate them to the development of virtues in his life.

We should not make the mistake of assuming that the Golden Rule, in whatever forms and expressions it may take, does away with the need for a moral code; it cannot replace other, related moral rules, standards and principles. In none of its formulations does the Rule answer the purpose of a complete system of morality. Each statement of it needs to be treated in the light of other moral values that we uphold. We have also noted that many statements of the Rule directly relate it to other moral values and, in fact, often appear inseparable from them. Nor would the Rule, we think, provide a person complete guidance for his moral development – moral education includes far more than the teaching and learning of the various examples of the Rule, but the Rule seems so fundamental that it cannot be excluded from such education.

On the other hand, the immense importance and high status of the Rule can never be overestimated. The great value placed upon the Rule may be explained from several perspectives. First is the widespread religious motivation that undergirds it. In this irreligious age we often neglect the fact that religion has proven, historically, to be a powerful and influential moral force indeed, and when religion throughout the world is revitalised that power and influence can be operative again. We have found that the Rule is likely to be found in the form of sayings in at least some traditional religions associated with small-scale societies. In addition, even in traditional societies that may not possess Golden Rule statements – written or oral, in the form of sayings, proverbs or portions of folktales – the principle of reciprocity, which is so fundamentally linked with the Rule, is practised in connection with religious beliefs. Further, we have noted how widespread the Rule is in the literature of the major religions of the world. Whether we regard each and all of the religions treated in this study as revealed and true or not, the fact remains that we have found more than one written statement of the Rule in nearly all, a further indication of how fundamental it is. In various cases, the great significance of the Rule is indicated in these statements. For instance, in the *Mahābhārata* of the Hindus we read:

> Do not to others what ye do not wish
> Done to yourself; and wish for others too
> – What ye desire and long for, for yourself
> – This is the whole of Dharma, heed it well.

And in the potent words of Jesus Christ in the Christian Bible:

> Therefore all things whatsoever ye would that men should do to you, do ye even so to them; for this is the law and the prophets.

And Bahá'u'lláh has written in *The Hidden Words*, referred to by him as '. . . that which hath descended from the Realm of Glory, uttered by the tongue of power and might, and revealed unto the Prophets of old':

> O Son of Being!
>   Ascribe not to any soul that which thou wouldst not have ascribed to thee, and say not that which thou doest not. This is My command unto thee, do thou observe it.

We have noted the considerable number of examples of the Rule at the high level of the principle of universal unrequiting goodness or the Rule of Love in religious literature, especially in the Bahá'í writings. We have proposed that this modern emphasis on the Rule of Love is a call to humanity to live up to the Golden Rule on a higher level than ever before, as well as to attain a higher standard of morality. The present writer feels that since the Rule is found so commonly, and at times is given such emphasis, among the world's religions, this is an indication how fundamental it is among the principles and teachings of religion itself as well as in religious and moral education. In some cases in the literature of the world's religions the source of the Rule may be traced to the Almighty. For instance, in the book of Leviticus in the Bible we find these powerful words:

Thou shalt love thy neighbour as thyself: I am the Lord.

The Rule has been passed down to man through numerous individuals who are regarded as divinely inspired founders of the great religions of the world, as prophets or messengers of God. Thus the power of divine authority is often associated with the Rule. In other cases, as in Jainism or Confucianism, no claim is made of a divine source for the Rule, but great respect is given to the individual or individuals who may have been the source of it. The question remains whether the teaching of the Rule from so many sources throughout the centuries has been, in reality, part of a unified effort within a wider, divine plan. Is *this* why the Rule has been so widespread among so many peoples and religions and has been enunciated by so many philosophers and sages? For there is power and purpose in unified, persistent action.

Other religious dimensions of the Rule underlie its significance for man. We have noted that, as indicated in some religious teachings, the Rule apparently plays an important role in the preparation of man for the next life and that reciprocal relationships can exist between souls both in this world and the next. We have, in fact, discovered that the context for our understanding of the Rule can be the whole of reality as encompassing 'three worlds': the world of God, the world of Manifestation, and the world of the created.

Not only is the Rule of prime significance in religion now, it can be such far into the future. The present writer has speculated on the possibility that the Rule could be brought by a future Manifestation or Manifestations. He has also investigated the question of the universal operation of the Rule throughout the universe far beyond our tiny planet and a limited time span.

It is the writer's view that although the varied formulations of the Rule do not answer the purpose of a complete system of morality, and cannot replace other moral values, the importance of these statements for moral development is largely due to their dynamic interaction with the development of many other moral values such as becoming loving or becoming just. He feels that it is not just a coincidence that statements of the Rule often directly link it to such virtues and qualities. For example, in the words of 'Abdu'l-Bahá:

Justice is not limited, it is a universal quality. Its operation must be carried out in all classes, from the highest to the lowest. Justice must be sacred, and the rights of all the people must be considered. Desire for others only that which you desire for yourselves. Then shall we rejoice in the Sun of Justice, which shines from the Horizon of God.[1]

We also saw how the words of Bahá'u'lláh in *The Hidden Words*, 'Ascribe not to any soul that which thou wouldst not have ascribed to thee' throw light upon the prohibitions against calumny and backbiting found in Bahá'u'lláh's *Kitáb-i-Aqdas* (The Book of Laws) and vice versa. In fact, we have investigated several significant instances of relationships between the Rule and law in Hinduism, Zoroastrianism, Judaism, Christianity and the Bahá'í Faith.

The role and importance of the Rule in religious and moral education in the past and present has been treated briefly here and there in this book. We have seen how very wide can be our view of the possible scope of education, and what significance this can have for our understanding of the use of the Rule in education. The schools are only one means through which the Rule can be taught and learned; parents obviously play a key role. The writer has pondered upon the possible teaching and learning of the Rule within a future universal education and universal curriculum, and of its being one of those 'principles of religion' that would be taught in the schools of the world 'in such a manner that it may not injure the children by resulting in ignorant fanaticism and bigotry'. If this were to happen, what would be the repercussions for the moral development of the whole human race?

We may investigate from another point of view why such great value has been and is placed on the Rule. The general acceptance, demonstrated value and universality of the Rule (although mere acceptance does not automatically guarantee conscientious practice) also underlie its fundamental importance to man. A prime reason for its general acceptance has already been referred to: its widespread existence and the emphasis it has been given among the world's religions. Secondly, its value can be proven by experience, an experience that mankind has shared through the centuries. ' . . . It is based on reasoning of the best way of living with others.'[2] We can use it successfully in its various versions over and over again in our everyday lives and rely on it in typical cases. The philosopher Paul Weiss stated:

Mankind with considerable ease seems to know how to use the Golden Rule, with its supposition that we can understand what it is to be in the position of another . . . There are no exceptions to the acceptance of the Golden Rule.[3]

He also wrote:

[The Golden Rule] is part of the inheritance of the West as well as of the East; yet it is affirmed and discovered anew in every generation and by almost every individual . . .[4]

This process can have a powerful effect on a person and his attainment of a higher degree of civilised conduct. Meng Tzŭ demonstrated penetrating insight when he declared:

If one strives to treat others as he would be treated by them he will come near the perfect life.

An individual can try to apply one or more statements of the
Rule day after day, year after year, and see what changes
take place in his life and, sooner or later, in the lives of
others. Maturation of moral conduct would most likely
take place. The process can also involve a profound
emotional concern for others, such as the underprivileged
or the members of one's family.

The term 'universality' of the Rule has various meanings.
The Rule, it has been stated over and over again, ultimately
should apply universally. Formulations of it are to be found
among the peoples of all races. It is part of the wide range of
experiences common to all people. It knows no colour bar.
It could apply to everyone: enemies, aliens, foreigners, as
well as those dear to us. In the writer's view, it can possess a
powerful appeal to those who are described in Bahá'í literature as lovers of the whole human race.

This book has attempted to demonstrate that the Rule is
directed to the whole of humanity: rulers and ruled, rich
and poor, philosophers and children just learning to read.
But its impact has varied from individual to individual. For
example, recent research among certain schoolchildren in
England indicates that few of those interviewed knew what
the Golden Rule is (most probably the Rule as known in
Christianity). Despite Weiss's view that there are no exceptions to the acceptance of the Golden Rule, some people
possess a negative attitude towards statements of it. One
writer referred to

. . . the logic-chopping, complicated, uninspired and uninspir-
ing epigram called the Golden Rule: 'Do unto others as you
would they should do unto you,' which to me personally is and
always has been perfectly meaningless.[5]

On the other hand, we have given examples of practice of
the Rule on a high level by religiously inspired persons at
various points in history – specifically, the practice of

universal unrequiting goodness or the Rule of Love, in which hatred, persecution, the murder of loved ones, and even impending death at the hands of opposers is reciprocated with love and forgiveness. Just as the impact of the Golden Rule on the masses of humanity has varied, so has its impact on the philosophers, seers and leaders of the world. The view has been presented that the source of this influence could clearly be traced in many instances to Manifestations of God such as Jesus Christ. The list of philosophers and other prominent figures who have made statements of the Rule in one form or another throughout history includes Epictetus, Herodotus, Isocrates, Plato, Aristotle, Thales, Seneca, Meng Tzŭ, Philo, Clement, St Augustine, Maimonides, Wang Yang-ming, Thomas Hobbes, John Stuart Mill, Immanuel Kant, Lord Chesterfield and Woodrow Wilson. Such persons, in turn, influence others. The philosopher John Stuart Mill considered the Golden Rule a valuable guide. Immanuel Kant, who perhaps possessed the most powerful and original mind in modern Western philosophy, was definitely influenced by the Rule. In *The Fundamental Principles of the Metaphysics of Morals*, the Calvinist Kant formulated and defended a general principle about right actions, essentially the following:

Suppose a man is considering whether it would be right for him to perform an action of the kind A in circumstances which, as he sees matters, are BCD. Then, Kant says, doing A is morally permissible (right) if the man is willing for *everyone* to make it a rule to do A in circumstances BCD. Otherwise it is wrong and the man's duty to avoid it. This is the principle of duty, 'the categorical imperative'. Kant conceived that it is part of rationality to refrain from conduct which one would not be willing to have made the universal rule . . .

There are various historical influences apparent in Kant's theory: the Golden Rule [we assume primarily the Christian formulations], Stoicism, eighteenth-century enthusiasm for being rational.[6]

In fact, even among materialist philosophers concerned with morality the Golden Rule has met with acceptance. Thomas Hobbes, the founder of the empirical tradition in English philosophy, approved of the Rule. This illustrates further the universality of the Rule to morality. (Could a materialist philosopher unknowingly participate in the unfoldment of a divine plan?) We have also noted in this study that the Rule can become known to people who may even be unaware of its close ties with various religions.

Historically, the impact of the Rule on the rulers of the world would again appear to be varied, but limited. Apparently a few took it seriously. 'The [Roman] Emperor Severus inscribed the rule on his palace walls, and perhaps doomed his palace thus, had he understood.'[7] From the ancient past, the author of the *Letter of Aristeas* advised a king:

As thou desirest that evils not befall thee, but to partake of all that is good, thou shouldst act in this spirit to thy subjects and to offenders, and shouldst very gently admonish such as are virtuous; for God draws all men (to Him) by gentleness.

How many rulers have paid heed to such words? But Bahá'u'lláh foretells that great rulers in the future will exemplify the Rule in their lives:

Erelong will God make manifest on earth kings who will recline on the couches of justice, and will rule amongst men even as they rule their own selves. They, indeed, are among the choicest of My creatures in the entire creation.

And what of the masses of mankind? Will they in future also exemplify the Rule in their lives to a much greater degree than we, 'the children of the half-light'? Will they respond to the exhortation to live up to a higher standard of morality?

We end this exploration of the boundless worlds of the Golden Rule with a prayer from the pen of Bahá'u'lláh:

Say: O God, my God! Attire mine head with the crown of justice, and my temple with the ornament of equity. Thou, verily, art the Possessor of all gifts and bounties.[8]

The end is merely a beginning.

Appendix

From the Writings of Bahá'u'lláh

O my brother! A divine Mine only can yield the gems of divine knowledge, and the fragrance of the mystic Flower can be inhaled only in the ideal Garden, and the lilies of ancient wisdom can blossom nowhere except in the city of a stainless heart. 'In a rich soil, its plants spring forth abundantly by permission of its Lord, and in that soil which is bad, they spring forth but scantily.'*

Inasmuch as it hath been clearly shown that only those who are initiated into the divine mysteries can comprehend the melodies uttered by the Bird of Heaven, it is therefore incumbent upon every one to seek enlightenment from the illumined in heart and from the Treasuries of divine mysteries regarding the intricacies of God's Faith and the abstruse allusions in the utterances of the Day-springs of Holiness. Thus will these mysteries be unravelled, not by the aid of acquired learning, but solely through the assistance of God and the outpourings of His grace. 'Ask ye, therefore, of them that have the custody of the Scriptures, if ye know it not.'†

But, O my brother, when a true seeker determines to take the step of search in the path leading to the knowledge of the Ancient of Days, he must, before all else, cleanse and purify his heart, which is the seat of the revelation of the inner mysteries of God, from the obscuring dust of all

* Qur'án 7:57.
† Qur'án 16:43.

acquired knowledge, and the allusions of the embodiments of satanic fancy. He must purge his breast, which is the sanctuary of the abiding love of the Beloved, of every defilement, and sanctify his soul from all that pertaineth to water and clay, from all shadowy and ephemeral attachments. He must so cleanse his heart that no remnant of either love or hate may linger therein, lest that love blindly incline him to error, or that hate repel him away from the truth. Even as thou dost witness in this day how most of the people, because of such love and hate, are bereft of the immortal Face, have strayed far from the Embodiments of the divine mysteries, and, shepherdless, are roaming through the wilderness of oblivion and error. That seeker must at all times put his trust in God, must renounce the peoples of the earth, detach himself from the world of dust, and cleave unto Him Who is the Lord of Lords. He must never seek to exalt himself above any one, must wash away from the tablet of his heart every trace of pride and vainglory, must cling unto patience and resignation, observe silence, and refrain from idle talk. For the tongue is a smouldering fire, and excess of speech a deadly poison. Material fire consumeth the body, whereas the fire of the tongue devoureth both heart and soul. The force of the former lasteth but for a time, whilst the effects of the latter endure a century.

That seeker should also regard backbiting as a grievous error, and keep himself aloof from its dominion, inasmuch as backbiting quencheth the light of the heart, and extinguish the life of the soul. He should be content with little, and be free from all inordinate desire. He should treasure the companionship of those that have renounced the world, and regard avoidance of boastful and worldly people a precious benefit. At the dawn of every day he should commune with God, and with all his soul persevere in the quest of his Beloved. He should consume every wayward thought with the flame of His loving mention, and, with the swiftness of lightning, pass by all else save Him. He should succour the dispossessed, and never withhold his favour from the destitute. He should show kindness to animals, how much more unto his fellow-man, to him who is endowed with the power of utterance. He should not hesitate to offer up his life for his Beloved, nor allow the censure of the people to turn him away from the Truth. He should not wish for others that which he doth not wish for himself, nor promise that which he doth not fulfil. With all his heart should the seeker avoid fellowship with evil doers, and pray for the remission of their sins. He should forgive the sinful, and never despise his low estate, for none knoweth what his own end shall be. How often hath a sinner, at the hour of death, attained to the essence of faith, and quaffing the immortal draught, hath taken his flight unto the celestial Concourse. And how often hath a devout believer, at the hour of his soul's ascension, been so changed as to fall into the nethermost fire. Our purpose in revealing these convincing and weighty utterances is to impress upon the seeker that he should regard all else beside God as transient, and count all things save Him, Who is the Object of all adoration, as utter nothingness.

These are among the attributes of the exalted, and constitute the hall-mark of the spiritually-minded. They have already been mentioned in connection with the requirements of the wayfarers that tread the Path of Positive Knowledge. When the detached wayfarer and sincere seeker hath fulfilled these essential conditions, then and only then can he be called a true seeker. Whensoever he hath fulfilled the conditions implied in the verse: 'Whoso maketh efforts for Us',* he shall enjoy the blessing conferred by the words: 'In Our ways shall We assuredly guide him.'†

Bahá'u'lláh, *Kitáb-i-Íqán*, pp. 122–3.

* Qur'án 29:69.
† Ibid.

From a Talk Given by 'Abdu'l-Bahá at the Second Divine Science Church, Denver, Colorado, 25 September 1912

One of the forms of prejudice which afflict the world of mankind is religious bigotry and fanaticism. When this hatred burns in human hearts, it becomes the cause of revolution, destruction, abasement of humankind and deprivation of the mercy of God. For the holy Manifestations and divine Founders of religion Themselves were completely unified in love and agreement, whereas Their followers are characterized by bitter antagonism and attitudes of hostility toward each other. God has desired for mankind the effulgence of love, but through blindness and misapprehension man has enveloped himself in veils of discord, strife and hatred. The supreme need of humanity is cooperation and reciprocity. The stronger the ties of fellowship and solidarity amongst men, the greater will be the power of constructiveness and accomplishment in all the planes of human activity. Without cooperation and reciprocal attitude the individual member of human society remains self-centered, uninspired by altruistic purposes, limited and solitary in development like the animal and plant organisms of the lower kingdoms. The lower creatures are not in need of cooperation and reciprocity. A tree can live solitary and alone, but this is impossible for man without retrogression. Therefore, every cooperative attitude and activity of human life is praiseworthy and foreintended by the will of God. The first expression of cooperation is family relationship, which is unreliable and uncertain in its potency, for it is subject to separation and does not permanently cement together the individual members of humanity. There is also a cooperation and oneness in nativity or race which is likewise not efficient, for although its members may agree in general, they differ radically in personal and particular points of view. Racial association, therefore, will not insure the requirements of divine relationship. There are other means in the human world by which physical association is established, but these fail to weld together the hearts and spirits of men and are correspondingly inefficient. Therefore, it is evident that God has destined and intended religion to be the cause and means of cooperative effort and accomplishment among mankind. To this end He has sent the Prophets of God, the holy Manifestations of the Word, in order that the fundamental reality and religion of God may prove to be the bond of human unity; for the divine religions revealed by these holy Messengers have one and the same foundation. All will admit, therefore, that the divine religions are intended to be the means of true human cooperation; that they are united in the purpose of making humanity one family, for they rest upon the universal foundation of love, and love is the first effulgence of Divinity.

'Abdu'l-Bahá, *The Promulgation of Universal Peace*,
pp. 337–8.

Bibliography

Aarne, Antti. *The Types of the Folktale: A Classification and Bibliography*. Trans. and enlarged by Stith Thompson. Helsinki: Suomalainen Tiedeakatemia Academia Scientiarum Fennica, 1973.

'Abdu'l-Bahá. *Foundations of World Unity*. Wilmette: Bahá'í Publishing Trust, 1945.

— *Paris Talks*. London: Bahá'í Publishing Trust, 1969.

— *The Promulgation of Universal Peace*. Talks Delivered by 'Abdu'l-Bahá During His Visit to the United States and Canada in 1912. Comp. Howard MacNutt. Wilmette: Bahá'í Publishing Trust, 1982.

— *Selections from the Writings of 'Abdu'l-Bahá*. Trans. by a Committee and by Marzieh Gail. Haifa: Bahá'í World Centre, 1978.

— *Some Answered Questions*. Wilmette: Bahá'í Publishing Trust, rev. edn 1981.

Ameer-'Ali, Syed. *The Spirit of Islam*. London: Christopher, 1922.

Báb, The. *Selections from the Writings of the Báb*. Haifa: Bahá'í World Centre, 1976.

Bahá'í Prayers. London: Bahá'í Publishing Trust, 1967.

Bahá'u'lláh. *Epistle to the Son of the Wolf*. Trans. Shoghi Effendi. Wilmette: Bahá'í Publishing Trust, 1938.

— *Gleanings from the Writings of Bahá'u'lláh*. Trans. Shoghi Effendi. London: Bahá'í Publishing Trust, 1949.

— *The Hidden Words*. Trans. Shoghi Effendi. New Delhi: Bahá'í Publishing Trust, 1973.

— *Kitáb-i-Íqán*. *The Book of Certitude*. Trans. Shoghi Effendi. London: Bahá'í Publishing Trust, 1961.

— *Prayers and Meditations by Bahá'u'lláh*. Trans. Shoghi Effendi. Wilmette: Bahá'í Publishing Trust, 1962.

— *The Proclamation of Bahá'u'lláh*. Haifa: Bahá'í World Centre, 1964.

— *Tablets of Bahá'u'lláh*. Trans. Habib Taherzadeh et al. Haifa: Bahá'í World Centre, 1978.

Baier, Kurt. *The Moral Point of View*. Ithaca, New York: Cornell University Press, 1958.

Balyuzi, H. M. *'Abdu'l-Bahá: The Centre of the Covenant of Bahá'u'lláh*. Oxford: George Ronald, 1971.
— *Bahá'u'lláh*. London: George Ronald, 1963.
— *Muḥammad and the Course of Islám*. Oxford: George Ronald, 1976.
Barclay, William. *Ethics in a Permissive Society*. London: Collins, 1971.
Berkouwer, G. C. *General Revelation*. Grand Rapids, Michigan: Wm. B. Eerdmans, 1955.
Bligh, John. *The Sermon on the Mount*. Slough, England: St Paul Publications, 1975.
Blyth, R. H. *Zen in English Literature and Oriental Classics*. Tokyo: The Hokuseido Press, 1942.
Bode, Dastur Framroze Ardeshir and Piloo Nanarutty (trans.). *Songs of Zarathustra: The Gathas*. London: Allen & Unwin, 1952.
Bradley, F. H. *Appearance and Reality*. Oxford: Clarendon Press, 1893.
Brandon, S. G. F. (ed.). *A Dictionary of Comparative Religion*. New York: Scribner, 1970.
Brandt, Richard B. *Value and Obligation: Systematic Readings in Ethics*. New York: Harcourt, Brace & World, 1961.
Brightman, F. E. 'Terms of Communion and the Ministration of the Sacraments in Early Times', in Swete, *Essays on the Early History of the Church*, q.v.
Bull, Norman J. *Moral Education*. London: Routledge & Kegan Paul, 1969.
— *Moral Judgement from Childhood to Adolescence*. London: Routledge & Kegan Paul, 1969.
Burtt, E. A. (ed.). *The Teachings of the Compassionate Buddha*. New York: New American Library, 1955.
Buttrick, G. A. (ed.). *The Interpreter's Bible*. Nashville, Tennessee: Abingdon Press, 1952.
Ching, Julia (trans.). *The Philosophical Letters of Wang Yang-ming*. Columbia, South Carolina: University of South Carolina, 1972.
Cole, W. Owen, and Piara Singh Sambhi. *The Sikhs: Their Religious Beliefs and Practices*. London: Routledge & Kegan Paul, 1978.
Conze, Edward. *Buddhism: Its Essence and Development*. Oxford: Bruno Cassirer, 1951.
Cunliffe-Jones, H. *Deuteronomy: Introduction and Commentary*. London: S.C.M. Press, 1951.
Dās, Bhagavān. *Essential Unity of All Religions*. Madras: The Theosophical Publishing House, 1955.
Diamond, Bernard L. 'Failures of Identification and Sociopathic Behavior', in Sanford et al., *Sanctions for Evil*, q.v.

Donaldson, Dwight M. *Studies in Muslim Ethics*. London: S.P.C.K., 1963.

Eliade, Mircea, and Joseph M. Kitawaga (eds.). *The History of Religions: Essays in Methodology*. Chicago: University of Chicago Press, 1959.

Erny, Pierre. *The Child and His Environment in Black Africa*. Trans. and abridged G. J. Wanjohi. Nairobi: Oxford University Press, 1981.

Esslemont, J. E. *Bahá'u'lláh and the New Era*. Wilmette, Bahá'í Publishing Trust, 1970.

Farsi, S. S. *Swahili Sayings from Zanzibar*. Vol. 1. *Proverbs*. Nairobi: Kenya Literature Bureau, 1958.

Feibleman, James K. *Understanding Philosophy*. London: Souvenir, 1973.

Ferm, Vergilius (ed.). *Encyclopedia of Morals*. London: Peter Owen, 1957.

Ferraby, John. *All Things Made New: A Comprehensive Outline of the Bahá'í Faith*. London: Bahá'í Publishing Trust, rev. edn 1975.

Furútan, A. A. *Mothers, Fathers and Children: Practical Advice to Parents*. Oxford: George Ronald, 1980.

Gibb, H. A. R., and J. H. Kramers. *Shorter Encyclopaedia of Islam*. Leiden: E. J. Brill, 1961.

Glatzer, Nahum H. (ed. and trans.). *The Judaic Tradition*. Boston: Beacon Press, 1969.

Graham, A. C. 'Confucianism', in R. C. Zaehner (ed.), *The Concise Encyclopaedia of Living Faiths*. London: Hutchinson, 1971.

Green, Ronald M. *Religious Reason: The Rational and Moral Basis of Religious Belief*. New York: Oxford University Press, 1978.

Gulpáygání, Mírzá Abu'l-Faḍl. *The Brilliant Proof*. Sydney, Australia: National Spiritual Assembly of the Bahá'ís of Australia and New Zealand, 1949.

Hammond, Phillip E., and Kirk R. Williams. 'Moral Climates of Nations: Measurement and Classification', in Robert Wuthnow (ed.), *The Religious Dimension: New Directions in Quantitative Research*. New York: Academic Press, 1979.

Heiler, Friedrich. 'The History of Religions as a Preparation for the Co-operation of Religions', in Mircea Eliade and Joseph M. Kitagawa, q. v.

von Hildebrand, Dietrich. *Ethics*. Chicago: Franciscan Herald Press, 1953.

Honnold, Annamarie (comp.). *Vignettes from the Life of 'Abdu'l-Bahá*. Oxford: George Ronald, 1982.

Hornby, Helen (comp.). *Lights of Guidance: A Bahá'í Reference File.* New Delhi: Bahá'í Publishing Trust, 1983.

Hoskyns, Sir Edwyn, and Noel Davy. *The Riddle of the New Testament.* London: Faber, 1958.

Hume, Robert Ernest. *The World's Living Religions.* New York: Scribner, 1959.

Huxley, Thomas H. *Evolution and Ethics and Other Essays.* London: Macmillan, 1894.

Idowu, E. Bọlaji. *Olódumarè: God in Yoruba Belief.* London, Longman, 1962.

Jain, Jyoti Prasad. 'Jainism', in *Way to Peace*, q.v.

Kateregga, Badru D., and David W. Shenk. *Islam and Christianity: A Muslim and a Christian in Dialogue.* Nairobi: Uzima Press, 1980.

King, George Brockwell. 'The "Negative" Golden Rule,' *Journal of Religion*, 8:270, 1928.

Lanczkowski, Günter. *Sacred Writings: A Guide to the Literature of Religions.* London: Collins, 1961.

Legge, James (trans.). *Confucius: Confucian Analects, The Great Learning and the Doctrine of the Mean.* New York: Dover, 1971.

Ling, Trevor. *A History of Religions East and West.* London: Macmillan, 1963.

McArthur, Harvey K. 'Golden Rule', in Macquarrie (ed.), *A Dictionary of Christian Ethics.* London: S.C.M. Press, 1967.

Macmurray, John. *Persons in Relation.* London: Faber, 1961.

Manson, T. W. *The Sayings of Jesus.* London: S.C.M. Press, 1949.

Maududi, Abul A'la. *Towards Understanding Islam.* Nairobi: The Islamic Foundation, 1973.

Mbiti, David M. *Foundations of School Administration.* Nairobi: Oxford University Press, 1974.

Mbiti, John S. *The Prayers of African Religion.* London: S.P.C.K., 1975.

Müller, F. Max (ed.). *The Sacred Books of the East.* New Delhi: Motilal Banarsidass.

> Vol. XVIII. *Pahlavi Texts.* Trans. E. W. West. *Part II: The Dādistān-ī Dīnīk and the Epistles of Mānūśkīhar.* 1882.

> Vol. XXIV. *Pahlavi Texts.* Trans. E. W. West. *Part III: Dīnā-ī Maīnög-i Khirad; Sikand-Gümānīk Vigar; Sad Dar.* 1885.

> Vol. XXVIII. *The Sacred Books of China: The Texts of Confucianism.* Trans. James Legge. *Part IV: The Lī Kī, XI-XLVII.* 1885.

> Vol. XXXVIII. *Pahlavi Texts.* Trans. E. W. West. *Contents of the Nasks.* 1892.

Vol. XXXIX. *The Sacred Books of China: The Texts of Taoism.* Trans. James Legge. *Part I: The Tao Teh King: The Writings of Kwang-Zze, Books I-XVII.* 1891.

Mwangi, Rose. *Kikuyu Folktales.* Nairobi: East African Literature Bureau, 1970.

Nabíl-i-A'zam (Muḥammad-i-Zarandí). *The Dawn-Breakers: Nabíl's Narrative of the Early Days of the Bahá'í Revelation.* Wilmette: Bahá'í Publishing Trust, 1932.

An-Nawawī's Forty Hadith. Trans. Ezeddin Ibrahim and Denys Johnson-Davies. Damascus: The Holy Koran Publishing House, 1976.

Nigosian, S. A. *World Religions.* London: Edward Arnold, 1975.

di Nola, A. M. (ed.). *The Prayers of Man.* London: Heinemann, 1962.

Noth, Martin. *Exodus: A Commentary.* London: S.C.M. Press, 1962.

Pauling, Linus. 'World Morality and World Peace'. *The Emerging World: Jawaharlal Nehru Memorial Volume.* Bombay: Asia Publishing House, 1964.

Pike, E. R. *Encyclopaedia of Religion and Religions.* London: Allen & Unwin, 1951.

Prasad Jain, Jyoti. 'Jainism', in *Way to Peace.* Lucknow: The Lucknow Publishing House, 1981.

Principles of Bahá'í Administration. London: Bahá'í Publishing Trust, 3rd edn 1973.

Rost, H. T. D. 'The Possible Nature and Establishment of Bahá'í Universities and Colleges Based Upon a Study of Bahá'í Literature'. Ann Arbor, Michigan: University Microfilms, 1970.

Sandmel, Samuel. *We Jews and Jesus.* London: Victor Gollancz, 1965.

Sanford, Nevitt, Craig Comstock et. al. (eds.). *Sanctions for Evil: Sources of Social Destructiveness.* Boston: Beacon Press, 1971.

Sears, William. *Thief in the Night.* London: George Ronald, 1961.

Shermis, S. Samuel. *Philosophic Foundations of Education.* New York: Van Nostrand Reinhold, 1967.

Shoghi Effendi. *The Advent of Divine Justice.* Wilmette: Bahá'í Publishing Trust, 1969.

— *Call to the Nations: Extracts from the Writings of Shoghi Effendi.* Haifa: Bahá'í World Centre, 1977.

— *God Passes By.* Wilmette: Bahá'í Publishing Trust, 1965.

— *Letters from the Guardian to Australia and New Zealand 1923–1957.* Sydney, Australia: National Spiritual Assembly of the Bahá'ís of Australia, 1970.

— *The Promised Day Is Come.* Wilmette: Bahá'í Publishing Trust, rev. edn 1980.

— *The World Order of Bahá'u'lláh*. Wilmette: Bahá'í Publishing Trust, 1980.

Shukla, J. D. 'Hinduism', in *Way to Peace*, q.v.

Sidgwick, Henry. *Outline of the History of Ethics for English Readers*. Boston: Beacon Press, 1960.

Singer, Marcus G. 'The Golden Rule', *Philosophy: The Journal of the Royal Institute of Philosophy*, 38:293–311, October 1963.

Singh, Gopal (trans.). *Sri Guru-Granth Sahib*. New York: Taplinger, n.d. Delhi: Gur Das Kapur, 1960 (?).

Smart, Ninian. 'Bhagavadgitā', in S. G. F. Brandon (ed.), *A Dictionary of Comparative Religion*. New York: Scribner, 1970.

Smith, J. W. D. *Religious Education in a Secular Setting*. London: S.C.M. Press, 1969.

Stutley, Margaret, and James Stutley. *A Dictionary of Hinduism*. London: Routledge & Kegan Paul, 1977.

Suda, J. P. *Religions in India: A Study of their Essential Unity*. New Delhi: Sterling, 1978.

Swete, H. B. (ed.). *Essays on the Early History of the Church and the Ministry by Various Writers*. London: Macmillan, 1918.

Synopsis and Codification of the Kitáb-i-Aqdas. Haifa: Bahá'í World Centre, 1973.

Taherzadeh, Adib. *The Revelation of Bahá'u'lláh: Baghdád 1853–63*. Oxford: George Ronald, 1974.

Tähtinen, Unto. *Ahiṃsā: Non-Violence in Indian Tradition*. London: Rider, 1976.

Taylor, W. S., and P. L. S. Taylor (eds.). *The Human Course: Collected Thoughts for Living*. New York: John Wiley, 1974.

Teilhard de Chardin, Pierre. *The Heart of Matter*. London: Collins, 1978.

Townshend, George. *The Heart of the Gospel*. London: George Ronald, 1951.

Universal House of Justice, The (comp.). *Living the Life*. New Delhi: Bahá'í Publishing Trust, n.d.

Way to Peace. Lucknow: The Lucknow Publishing House, 1981.

Weiss, Paul. 'The Golden Rule', *The Journal of Philosophy*, 38:421–31, July 1941.

— *Philosophy in Process*. Vol. 6: 28 August, 1968 – 22 May, 1971. Carbondale, Illinois: Southern Illinois University Press, 1975.

Werblowsky, R. J. Zwi. 'Judaism, or the Religion of Israel', in Zaehner (ed.), *The Concise Encyclopaedia of Living Faiths*. London: Hutchinson, 1971.

Wheelwright, Philip. *A Critical Introduction to Ethics*. New York: The Odyssey Press, 1935.

Yusuf Ali, Abdullah. *The Meaning of the Glorious Qur'án*. Cairo: Dar al-Kitab al-Masri, 1938.

Zaehner, R. C. *Hinduism*. Oxford: Oxford University Press, 1966.

— (ed.). *The Concise Encyclopaedia of Living Faiths*. London: Hutchinson, 1971.

References

INTRODUCTION

1 Shoghi Effendi, *The Promised Day Is Come*, pp. 114–15.
2 Smith, *Religious Education in a Secular Setting*, p. 63.

1. RELIGION, MORALITY AND ETHICS

1 Shermis, *Philosophic Foundations of Education*, p. 117.
2 From a letter written on behalf of Shoghi Effendi, 6 December
   1939. Cited in Hornby, *Lights of Guidance*, pp. 417–18.
3 Ferraby, *All Things Made New*, p. 108.
4 Bull, *Moral Judgement from Childhood to Adolescence*, pp. 32–3.
5 Bradley, *Appearance and Reality*, p. 381.
6 Teilhard de Chardin, *The Heart of Matter*, pp. 218, 220.
7 Hammond and Williams, 'Moral Climates of Nations . . .', p.
   312.

2. WHAT IS THE GOLDEN RULE?

1 *Confucian Analects*, Book XV, Chapter XXIII, in Legge,
   Confucius, p. 301.
2 McArthur, 'Golden Rule', p. 136.
3 Hume, *The World's Living Religions*, p. 278.
4 *Dīnkard*, Book VIII, Chapter XIX, in Müller, Vol. XXXVIII, p.
   51.
5 Singer, 'The Golden Rule', pp. 299–302.
6 Ibid. p. 294. Singer discusses this issue in detail on pp. 294–7,
   310–11.
7 *Mahābhārata*, Viḍura-nīti, cited in Bhagavān Dās, *Essential Unity
   of All Religions*, p. 410.
8 Feibleman, *Understanding Philosophy*, pp. 61–2.
9 Singer, pp. 294–5.
10 Ibid. p. 293.

3. COMPARATIVE RELIGION AND THE GOLDEN RULE

1 Bahá'u'lláh, *Tablets*, pp. 35–6.
2 Berkouwer, *General Revelation*, p. 155.
3 Ibid. pp. 160–61.
4 Hume, *The World's Living Religions*, pp. 270–82.
5 See, for example, Friedrich Heiler, 'The History of Religions as a
   Preparation for the Co-operation of Religions', pp. 132–60.
6 Huxley, *Evolution and Ethics*, p. 31.
7 MacMurray, *Persons in Relation*, pp. 62–3.

4. THE GOLDEN RULE IN TRADITIONAL RELIGIONS AND SOCIETIES

1 Erny, *The Child and His Environment in Black Africa*, p. 121.
2 Ibid. p. 124.
3 Ibid. p. 128.
4 Farsi, *Swahili Sayings from Zanzibar*, p. 2.
5 Written statement by Mr Barnabas Kipkorir, 1 July 1983.
6 Statement by Dr Kamuyu-wa-Kang'ethe, 11 July 1983.
7 Mwangi, *Kikuyu Folktales*, p. 44.
8 Aarne, *The Types of the Folktale*, p. 79.
9 E. Bọlaji Idowu, *Olódùmarà: God in Yoruba Belief*, p. 166.
10 A. M. di Nola (ed.), *The Prayers of Man* (London: Heinemann,
   1962), p. 23, cited in Mbiti, *The Prayers of African Religion*, p.
   97.
11 Written statement by Mr Joseph Sukwianomb, 30 April 1983.

5. IN HINDUISM

1 Ling, A *History of Religions East and West*, p. 142.
2 Zaehner, *Hinduism*, p. 2.
3 Ibid.
4 Potter, *Presuppositions of India's Philosophies*, p. 8, cited in Stutley
   and Stutley, *A Dictionary of Hinduism*. p. 76.
5 Shukla, 'Hinduism', p. 15.
6 Smart, 'Bhagavadgitā', p. 136.
7 Stutley and Stutley, p. 169.
8 *Mahābhārata*, cited in Dās, p. 398.
9 Zaehner, *Hinduism*, p. 126.
10 Stutley and Stutley, p. 236.
11 Zaehner, *Hinduism*, p. 126.
12 *Bhāgavata*, cited in Dās, p. 399.
13 Stutley and Stutley, p. 182.

14 Nigosian, *World Religions*, p. 108.
15 Stutley and Stutley, p. 182.
16 Ibid.
17 *Manu-smṛti*, cited in Dās, pp. 404–5.
18 Stutley and Stutley, p. 114.
19 *Hiṭ-opaḍésha*, cited in Dās, pp. 404–5.

6. IN JAINISM

1 Jain, 'Jainism', p. 52.
2 Ling, *A History of Religions East and West*, p. 99.
3 Tähtinen, *Ahiṃsā: Non-Violence in Indian Tradition*, p. 90.
4 Royston Pike, *Encyclopaedia of Religion and Religions*, p. 203.
5 Ibid.
6 Suda, *Religions in India*, pp. 203–4.
7 *Āchāra-aṅga-sūṭra*, 'Samaṭṭa', Chapter 4, Verse 2; *Āchāra-aṅga-sūṭra*, 'Loga-Sara', Chapter 5, Verse 5; cited in Dās, pp. 400–401.
8 *Yoga-Śāstra*, cited in Bull, *Moral Judgement*, p. 92.
9 Huxley, *Evolution and Ethics*, pp. 32–3.
10 'Abdu'l-Bahá, *Selections*, pp. 158–9.

7. IN BUDDHISM

1 Ling, *A History of Religions East and West*, p. 88.
2 Hume, *The World's Living Religions*, p. 78.
3 *Sigalovada Sutta*, 31, cited in Burtt, *The Teachings of the Compassionate Buddha*, p. 110.
4 *Majjhima Nikaya*, 1:415, as translated in Rhys Davids, *Buddhism*, p. 125. Cited in Hume, p. 277.
5 *Dhamma-pada*, cited in Dās, p. 406.
6 *Mataka-bhaṭṭa Jāṭaka*, cited in Dās, p. 403.
7 Conze, *Buddhism*, pp. 61–2.
8 Tähtinen, *Ahiṃsa*, p. 46.

8. IN TAOISM

1 Hume, *The World's Living Religions*, p. 131.
2 Ibid.
3 Ling, *A History of Religions East and West*, p. 109.
4 Hume, p. 133.
5 Ibid. p. 145.

6 *The Tâo Teh King*, Part II, Chapter 49, Verse 2, in Müller, Vol. XXXIX, p. 91.

7 *The Tao Teh King*, Part II, Chapter 63, Verse 1, in Müller, p. 106.

8 'Abdu'l-Bahá, *The Promulgation of Universal Peace*, p. 384.

9 Ameer-'Ali, *The Spirit of Islam*, p. 178.

10 Phelps, *Life and Teachings of Abbas Effendi*, cited in Balyuzi, *'Abdu'l-Bahá*, pp. 101–2.

11 Hume, p. 142.

12 *T'ai Shang Kan Ying P'ien*, cited in Dās, p. 405.

13 *T'ai Shang Kan Ying P'ien*, cited in Bull, p. 92.

9. IN CONFUCIANISM

1 Graham, 'Confucianism', in Zaehner, *The Concise Encyclopaedia of Living Faiths*, p. 358.

2 Hume, *The World's Living Religions*, p. 112.

3 Lanczkowski, *Sacred Writings*, p. 162.

4 *Confucian Analects*, Book XV, Chapter XXIII, in Legge, *Confucius*, p. 301.

5 Hume, p. 121.

6 Wang Yu-Po's paraphrase of the Sacred Edict of the Emperor Kang-hsi, in Legge, *Religions of China*, p. 105. Cited in Hume, p. 121.

7 The Lî Kî, Book XXXIX: *Tâ Hsio or The Great Learning*, in Müller, Vol. XXVIII, pp. 411, 419.

8 *The Doctrine of the Mean*, Chapter XIII, Verses 1, 3–4, in Legge, *Confucius*, pp. 393–5.

9 *Confucian Analects*, Book XII, Chapter II, in Legge, *Confucius*, p. 251.

10 *Confucian Analects*, Book V, Chapter XI, in Legge, *Confucius*, p. 177.

11 Mencius, cited in Taylor and Taylor, *The Human Course*, p. 15.

12 Ching, *The Philosophical Letters of Wang Yang-ming*, p. 17.

10. IN ZOROASTRIANISM

1 Ling, *A History of Religions East and West*, p. 75.

2 Zaehner, *Zurvan: A Zoroastrian Dilemma*, p. 4, cited in Ling, p. 77.

3 Ling, p. 77.

4 Zaehner, 'Zoroastrianism', pp. 213–14.

5 Hume, *The World's Living Religions*, p. 215.

6 Ling, p. 81.

7 Zaehner, 'Zoroastrianism', p. 212.
8 Gāthā, 43.1, cited in Dās, pp. 407–8.
9 Zaehner, 'Zoroastriansim', p. 209.
10 Dādistān-ī Dīnīk, Chapter XCIV, in Müller, Vol. XVIII, pp. 269, 271.
11 Dīnkard, Book VIII, Chapter XIX, in Müller, Vol. XXXVIII, p. 51.
12 Sad Dar, or The Hundred Subjects, Chapter LXV, in Müller, Vol. XXIV, pp. 329–30.
13 Weiss, 'The Golden Rule', p. 429.

11. IN JUDAISM

1 Ling, A History of Religions East and West, p. 18.
2 Ibid. p. 24.
3 Werblowsky, 'Judaism, or the Religion of Israel', p. 7.
4 Nigosian, World Religions, p. 30.
5 Ibid. pp. 34–5.
6 Lanczkowski, Sacred Writings, p. 107.
7 Noth, Exodus: A Commentary, p. 182.
8 Cunliffe-Jones, Deuteronomy: Introduction and Commentary, p. 118.
9 Bull, Moral Education, pp. 155–6.
10 Ibid. pp. 157–8.
11 Green, Religious Reason, p. 131.
12 Glatzer, The Judaic Tradition, p. 223.
13 Strack-Billerbeck, Kommentar zum Neuen Testament aus Talmud und Midrasch, I, 353–64, in King, 'The "Negative" Golden Rule', p. 278.
14 King, 'The "Negative" Golden Rule'.
15 Hume, The World's Living Religions, p. 194.
16 Werblowsky, p. 20.
17 Glatzer, p. 191.
18 Green, p. 131.
19 Shabbath 1, 31a, cited in Glatzer, p. 197.
20 Brandon, A Dictionary of Comparative Religion, p. 98.
21 Letter of Aristeas (Thackeray's translation), § 207, cited in Manson, The Sayings of Jesus, p. 52.

12. IN CHRISTIANITY

1 Lanczkowski, Sacred Writings, pp. 36–7.
2 Sidgwick, Outline of the History of Ethics, p. 109.

3 von Hildebrand, *Ethics*, p. 455.

4 Wheelwright, *A Critical Introduction to Ethics*, p. 153.

5 Hume, *The World's Living Religions*, p. 258.

6 Brightman, 'Terms of Communion . . .', p. 332.

7 King, 'The "Negative" Golden Rule', pp. 270–71.

8 Ibid. p. 272.

9 McArthur, 'Golden Rule', p. 136.

10 King, p. 274.

11 Hoskyns and Davy, *The Riddle of the New Testament*, p. 135.

12 Barclay, *Ethics in a Permissive Society*, pp. 39–40.

13 Gulpáygání, *The Brilliant Proof*. See also 'Abdu'l-Bahá, *Promulgation*, pp. 431–7, 453–7.

14 Qur'án, Súrihs 10:15 and 46:7–10.

15 Bahá'u'lláh, in *Bahá'í World Faith*, p. 55, and in *Gleanings*, pp. 102–3.

16 McArthur, 'Golden Rule', p. 137.

17 Bligh, *The Sermon on the Mount*, p. 150.

18 King, p. 275.

19 Ibid. pp. 275–7.

20 Singer, 'The Golden Rule', pp. 293–4, 304–6.

21 Manson, *The Sayings of Jesus*, p. 52.

22 Sandmel, *We Jews and Jesus*, p. 109.

23 Townshend, *The Heart of the Gospel*, pp. 114–15.

24 Max Müller, *Leben und Religion* (Stuttgart, n.d.), p. 153, cited in Heiler, 'The History of Religions as a Preparation for the Co-operation of Religions', p. 141.

25 Heiler, p. 135.

26 Shoghi Effendi, *The Advent of Divine Justice*, p. 14.

27 Written statement by Mr Ted Groenewegen, 24 May 1983.

28 Súrih 5:76–7 in Yusuf Ali, *The Meaning of the Glorious Qur'án*, Vol. I, p. 266.

29 'Abdu'l-Bahá, *Some Answered Questions*, pp. 113–15.

30 Ibid. p. 113.

31 Ibid. p. 114.

32 Súrih 42:13 in Yusuf Ali, Vol. II, p. 1308.

33 Súrih 2:106 in Yusuf Ali, Vol. I, pp. 46–7.

34 Shoghi Effendi, cited in 'Introduction', *Call to the Nations*, p. xi.

35 Shoghi Effendi, *The Promised Day Is Come*, p. 108.

36 Ibid. p. 118.

37 Shoghi Effendi, *Letters from the Guardian to Australia and New Zealand 1923–1957*, p. 41.

13. IN ISLÁM

1 Translation by A. J. Arberry.
2 Balyuzi, *Muḥammad and the Course of Islám*, p. 158.
3 Maududi, *Towards Understanding Islam*, p. 17.
4 Kateregga and Shenk, *Islam and Christianity: A Muslim and a Christian in Dialogue*, p. 71.
5 Maududi, p. 111.
6 Ibid.
7 Súrih 83: 1–6 in Yusuf Ali, *The Meaning of the Glorious Qur'án*, Vol. II, p. 1703.
8 Ibid.
9 Súrih 59:9 in Yusuf Ali, Vol. II, pp. 1523–4.
10 Gibb and Kramers, *Shorter Encyclopaedia of Islam*, p. 119.
11 *An-Nawawī's Forty Hadith*, p. 56.
12 *Sukhanán-i-Muḥammad*, Nos. 14, 21, 63, 306 (Teheran, 1938), cited in Donaldson, *Studies in Muslim Ethics*, p. 82.
13 Donaldson, p. 81.
14 Ibid. p. 122.
15 Ibid. p. 130.
16 From Ṣúfí writings, cited in Dās, *Essential Unity of All Religions*, p. 406.
17 *An-Nawawī's Forty Hadith*, p. 106.
18 Baier, *The Moral Point of View*, pp. 202–3.
19 See Singer, 'The Golden Rule', pp. 306–8.
20 Diamond, 'Failures of Identification and Sociopathic Behaviour', p. 126.
21 Ibid. pp. 128–9.
22 Ibid. pp. 134–5.
23 Bahá'u'lláh, *Tablets of Bahá'u'lláh*, p. 168.
24 Pauling, 'World Morality and World Peace', pp. 136–8, 146.

14. IN SIKHISM

1 Zaehner, *Hinduism*, p. 235.
2 Cole and Singh Sambhi, *The Sikhs*, p. 136.
3 Hume, *The World's Living Religions*, pp. 97–8.
4 Singh (trans.), *Sri Guru-Granth Sahib*, Vol. I, p. 250.
5 *Granṭh Sāhab*, 'Siḍh-gosht', cited in Dās, p. 403.
6 Kabír, cited in Bull, *Moral Judgement*, p. 92.

15. IN THE BAHÁ'Í FAITH: AN INTRODUCTION

1 In Taylor and Taylor, *The Human Course*, p. 583. After John Burroughs, *Accepting the Universe* (Houghton, 1920), p. 314.
2 Sarvepalli Radhakrishnan, cited in Nigosian, *World Religions*, p. 5.
3 See, for example, Sears, *Thief in the Night*.
4 'Abdu'l-Bahá, *Some Answered Questions*, pp. 39ff.
5 Ibid. p. 25.
6 Nabíl-i-A'zam, *The Dawn-Breakers*, p. 303.
7 Ibid. pp. 500–526.
8 The Báb, *Selections*, p. 129.
9 Introduction to *The Proclamation of Bahá'u'lláh*, p. ix.
10 Bahá'u'lláh, *Tablets*, pp. 88–9.
11 Shoghi Effendi, *God Passes By*, pp. 93–4.
12 See Shoghi Effendi, 'The Dispensation of Bahá'u'lláh' in *The World Order of Bahá'u'lláh*, p. 134.
13 Statement by Shoghi Effendi, in The Universal House of Justice, *Living the Life*, p. 38.
14 Ferraby, *All Things Made New*, p. 110.
15 'Abdu'l-Bahá, *Some Answered Questions*, p. 230.
16 Balyuzi, *Bahá'u'lláh*, p. 87.
17 'Abdu'l-Bahá, *Promulgation*, p. 159.
18 Bahá'u'lláh, *Gleanings*, p. 289.
19 'Abdu'l-Bahá, *Promulgation*, pp. 335–6.
20 'Abdu'l-Bahá, *Selections*, pp. 79–80.
21 'Abdu'l-Bahá, *Paris Talks*, p. 60.
22 'Abdu'l-Bahá, *Some Answered Questions*, p. 145.
23 'Abdu'l-Bahá, *Paris Talks*, p. 59.
24 'Abdu'l-Bahá, *Promulgation*, pp. 391–2.
25 Ibid. p. 152.
26 Bahá'u'lláh, *Epistle to the Son of the Wolf*, p. 13.
27 'Abdu'l-Bahá, *Promulgation*, pp. 337–8.
28 Shoghi Effendi, 'The Unfoldment of World Civilization' in *The World Order of Bahá'u'lláh*, p. 204.
29 'Abdu'l-Bahá, *Promulgation*, p. 102.
30 'Abdu'l-Bahá, *Paris Talks*, p. 82.
31 'Abdu'l-Bahá, *Promulgation*, p. 469.
32 Shoghi Effendi, 'The Golden Age of the Cause of Bahá'u'lláh', in *The World Order of Bahá'u'lláh*, pp. 60–61.
33 'Abdu'l-Bahá, *Selections*, p. 66.
34 'Abdu'l-Bahá, *Promulgation*, pp. 379–80.
35 Bahá'u'lláh, cited in *A Synopsis and Codification of the Kitáb-i-*

   Aqdas, pp. 27–8.
36 The Báb, *Selections*, p. 125.
37 Bahá'u'lláh, *Gleanings*, p. 65.
38 'Abdu'l-Bahá, *Some Answered Questions*, pp. 180–81.
39 Bahá'u'lláh, *Gleanings*, pp. 161–2.
40 'Abdu'l-Bahá, *Some Answered Questions*, p. 123.
41 Bahá'u'lláh, *Gleanings*, p. 162.
42 Ibid.
43 'Abdu'l-Bahá, *Selections*, p. 160.
44 'Abdu'l-Bahá, *Some Answered Questions*, pp. 245–7.
45 'Abdu'l-Bahá, *Promulgation*, p. 270.
46 'Abdu'l-Bahá, *Selections*, p. 48.
47 'Abdu'l-Bahá, *Some Answered Questions*, pp. 178–9.
48 'Abdu'l-Bahá, *Foundations of World Unity*, p. 63.
49 'Abdu'l-Bahá, *Paris Talks*, p. 16.

16. SOME GOLDEN RULE STATEMENTS IN THE BAHÁ'Í WRITINGS

1 Taherzadeh, *The Revelation of Bahá'u'lláh: Baghdád 1853–63*, p. 72.
2 Shoghi Effendi, *God Passes By*, p. 140.
3 Shoghi Effendi, 'The Dispensation of Bahá'u'lláh', in *The World Order of Bahá'u'lláh*, p. 131.
4 'Abdu'l-Bahá, *Promulgation*, p. 86.
5 Shoghi Effendi, *God Passes By*, p. 140.
6 Bahá'u'lláh, *The Hidden Words*, Arabic Nos. 26–9.
7 Esslemont, *Bahá'u'lláh and the New Era*, pp. 93–4.
8 Shoghi Effendi, *God Passes By*, pp. 138–9.
9 Shoghi Effendi, 'The Golden Age of the Cause of Bahá'u'lláh', in *The World Order of Bahá'u'lláh*, pp. 61–2.
10 Shoghi Effendi, *God Passes By*, p. 139.
11 Ibid.
12 Bahá'u'lláh, *Kitáb-i-Íqán*, pp. 123–5.
13 Shoghi Effendi, *God Passes By*, pp. 171–2.
14 Bahá'u'lláh, *Gleanings*, pp. 127–8.
15 Tablet of Bahá'u'lláh to Queen Victoria, cited in *The Proclamation of Bahá'u'lláh*, p. 12.
16 Bahá'u'lláh, Ridván-u'l-'Adl, cited in Shoghi Effendi, *The Promised Day Is Come*, p. 74.
17 Shoghi Effendi, *God Passes By*, p. 216.
18 Bahá'u'lláh, *Tablets*, p. 64.
19 Shoghi Effendi, *God Passes By*, p. 213.
20 Ibid. pp. 213–14.
21 Bahá'u'lláh, cited in *A Synopsis and Codification of the Kitáb-i-*

Aqdas, p. 13.
22 'Abdu'l-Bahá, cited in *Principles of Bahá'í Administration*, p. 52.
23 Bahá'u'lláh, *Prayers and Meditations*, pp. 81–2.
24 'Abdu'l-Bahá, *Paris Talks*, p. 66.
25 'Abdu'l-Bahá, *Some Answered Questions*, p. 232.
26 'Abdu'l-Bahá, *'Abdu'l-Bahá in London*, p. 97, cited in Honnold, *Vignettes*, p. 132.
27 'Abdu'l-Bahá, *Some Answered Questions*, p. 240.
28 'Abdu'l-Bahá, *Paris Talks*, pp. 159–60.
29 Singer, 'The Golden Rule', p. 302.
30 Bahá'u'lláh, *Tablets*, p. 71.
31 Bahá'u'lláh, *Gleanings*, p. 201.
32 'Abdu'l-Bahá, *Promulgation*, p. 453.
33 Ibid. p. 395.
34 Ibid. p. 218.

17. THE GOLDEN RULE AND THE EDUCATION OF MANKIND

1 'Abdu'l-Bahá, *Promulgation*, p. 330.
2 Letter from the Universal House of Justice to all National Spiritual Assemblies, 31 August 1976.
3 Bahá'u'lláh, *Tablets*, p. 68.
4 'Abdu'l-Bahá, *Promulgation*, p. 182.
5 Mbiti, *Foundations of School Administration*, p. 55.
6 Letter from Shoghi Effendi to an individual, 7 February 1947, cited in Rost, 'Bahá'í Universities and Colleges', p. 159.
7 Furútan, *Mothers, Fathers and Children*, pp. 256–9.
8 Singer, 'The Golden Rule', p. 310.
9 *Tobit* 4:14–15, cited in Hume, *The World's Living Religions*, p. 278.

18. THE FUNDAMENTAL IMPORTANCE OF THE GOLDEN RULE TO MAN

1 'Abdu'l-Bahá, *Paris Talks*, pp. 159–60.
2 Bull, *Moral Education*, p. 156.
3 Weiss, *Philosophy in Process*, Vol. 6, p. 345.
4 Weiss, 'The Golden Rule', p. 421.
5 Blyth, *Zen in English Literature and Oriental Classics*, p. 351.
6 Brandt, *Value and Obligation*, pp. 190–91.
7 Buttrick, *The Interpreter's Bible*, Vol. VII, p. 330.
8 *Bahá'í Prayers*, p. 12.